I0187163

Follow Norma's story from the beginning

Impressions Behind the Pink Ribbon

Writing Through the Laughter and Tears
with My Metastatic Breast Cancer

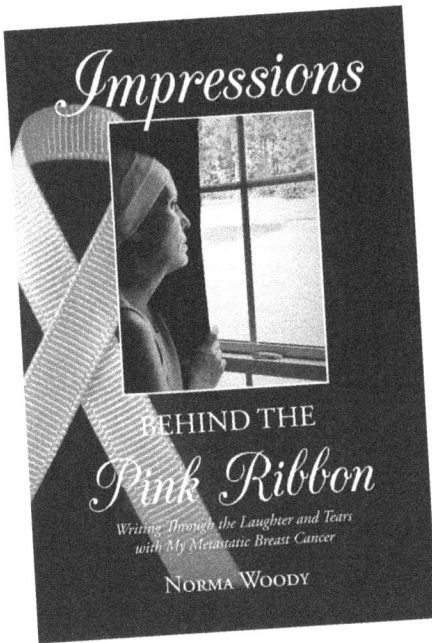

Order direct from amazon.com, from bn.com, from the publisher at www.belleislebooks.com, or from your favorite bookseller.

Impressions Beyond the Terminal Cancer Diagnosis

Impressions Beyond the Terminal Cancer Diagnosis

By Norma Woody

BELLE ISLE BOOKS
www.belleislebooks.com

Copyright 2020 by Norma Woody. No part of this book may be reproduced in any form or by any electronic or mechanical means, or the facilitation thereof, including information storage and retrieval systems, without permission in writing from the publisher, except in the case of brief quotations published in articles and reviews. Any educational institution wishing to photocopy part or all of the work for classroom use, or individual researchers who would like to obtain permission to reprint the work for educational purposes, should contact the publisher.

ISBN: 978-1-947860-46-9

Library of Congress Control Number 2019908356

Printed in the United States

Published by

BELLE ISLE BOOKS

www.belleislebooks.com

To all of the warriors who are fighting the battle.
To all of the families, friends, and caregivers
who give love and support during the battle.
And to all of those who rejoice or mourn the
outcome of the battle.

Author's Note

When I write, it is as if there is a party for stories going on in my head, and words are the confetti. I have a thought and then the words find their way into my developing story. They always seem to fall in place *just right* to describe what it is that I'm feeling. It's amazing that they are all around me waiting for me to harness them into my story like catching beautiful butterflies with a net from a massive endless swarm. There is a quest within my mind that never fails to satisfy my imagination. I am grateful for the ability to express that imagination along with my life stories.

CURRENTLYMYTIME
HASUNFORTUNATELYEVOLVED
INTOAPREOCCUPATIONOFTHOUGHTS
THATNOWCOEXISTWITHTHISNEWTAUNTING
OFMYMINDTOLETGOOFTHISFRAILFALTERINGLIFE
THATISSOODESPERATELYCLINGTO. INOWFINDMYSELF
UNDERSTANDABLYSTRUGGLINGWITHTHEFEARS
THATACCOMPANYITSPASSAGEANDTHEDAYS
INWHICHIHAVELIVEDANDIHAVELOVED
INTHISWORLD.TIMEHASBECOME
SOPRECIOUS.
WILL
WE
FIND
ANEWPEACE
WITHINOURSELVES
INOURUNDERSTANDINGTHAT
WHENTHISTIMEENDSOURETERNITYWILL
THENBEGINANDTIMEASWEKNOWITWILLBEFOR
USALLTOTALLYIRRELEVANTWITHNOMORECLOCKS
WATCHESORSCHEDULESTOKEEPONLYATRANQUILITY
THATHASBEENILLUSIVETOSOMANYTHROUGHOUT
OURENTIRELIFEHEREONEARTH.ONLYTHENWILL
WEFINALLYESCAPEALLOURBOUNDARIES
ANDOURSPIRITISFINALLYSETFREE
FORALLOFETERNITY

Contents

Acknowledgements

I would like to thank all of our family and friends. Without their love, prayers, visits, texts, and supportive calls, it would have been impossible for Norma and me to have fought this battle. I want to thank all of the prayer warriors, known and unknown to us, who were there for our family. I wish to give thanks to our Lord and Savior, who gave all of us the strength and hope during the fight, and for giving Norma the strength needed to finish this book. I also want to thank Dr. Lynne Einhaus, a family friend, for her support; Pastor Angie Frame for her support and prayers; and the entire team at St. Mary's Hospital, who showed such compassion, love, and kindness during the final days of Norma's life.

I also want to thank our publisher, Robert Pruett, for all of his help and insight in publishing Norma's books.

I want to personally thank Norma for the twenty years we shared. In her, I found what true love and friendship really is. She was an inspiration and joy to be with daily. She is truly missed.

Thank You, Darlin'…
Richard

In Her Own Words
How I Think While Fighting Terminal Cancer

Thoughts while fighting for one's life are far from stable. This book shows one woman's wide range of thoughts that are occupying her mind while trying to break past the odds that she can survive a three-month terminal cancer prognosis. Now approaching two years, she is releasing her second book that shares an array of emotions and discoveries that helped sustain her.

Until I take my last breath, I am a survivor, and I will ask that how I fight to survive be respected. After all, everyone makes decisions every day that succeed or fail, and navigating through cancer is no exception. Love and prayer will always go a lot further with this cancer patient than lofty or judgmental opinions.

That's my opinion.

Introduction

The first book I wrote was a collection of thoughts I had released on paper while I was suffering through cancer treatments. I now continue those thoughts in a sometimes stronger will, body, and outlook on life itself. Despite the fact that I am no longer fighting my cancer medically, I feel stronger. I have regained some of the strength lost while on chemo. And as strange as it may sound to some, my will has gained momentum with every month I am still alive.

I have learned so much more than I had anticipated while being thrust into this world of fighting for survival. I have learned a lot about human behavior, the world of medicine, and my own fears and emotions. All of these categories have let me down, surprised me, and strangely enough, even fulfilled me in the unexpected friendships that have developed.

When I was given approximately three months to live in October 2014, I was shocked, to say the least. I learned that the cancer inside me was not only growing; it was spreading. After my failed attempts to tolerate chemo treatments, I decided that I would trust in my own immune system and God to sustain me for as long as possible.

When the three months expired, and I didn't, I decided to plan for a future. Several people encouraged me to present the collection of my fluctuating thoughts to a publisher. And that I did. You see, my reasoning was that I could take the prognosis to heart and hit the bed of despair and let this three-month prediction come true, or I could ignore it to the best of my ability and see what could still be achieved in my limited life. Having my first manuscript accepted and published by the first publisher I presented it to was the diversion I needed to survive. And now, nineteen months later, I am ready to close out the completion of my second collection of thoughts.

I am not a conformist. I am creative in every aspect of my life. There is no greater evidence of this than in my writing. I write where my mind wanders. And believe me when I say that my mind does experience a lot of thoughts that are without boundaries. I write them down without any deviation from what they dictate to me.

This book is my collection of those thoughts as I rediscovered myself. I found that I had a greater sense of forgiveness than I thought. I also discovered I was capable of more than I ever imagined, and that I loved God more deeply than I realized.

I learned to appreciate everything around me on a higher level. I feel as if the closer I come to approaching death, the more heightened my senses become. I have always been sensitive to the life around me, but now there is a hunger for more. My eyes and mind seem to be acutely receptive to more than time allots me to inherit.

I am still alive and . . . well, read and see for yourself what my mind is up to now.

Forever does exist just beyond where I am now standing.

My Breast Cancer Story

To begin my story of living with breast cancer I must venture back to my childhood—a childhood where I lived what I thought was a normal life, as reserved as it was at times. I can remember feeling tired even in elementary school but accepted this feeling as how all humans felt, so I lived my life to the best of my abilities. My family of origin and I were plagued by many problems, both medical and in living life, but we all worked hard and made our way as best we could.

As I started maturing, I noticed my fatigue also matured. At this point in my life, I was still assuming that this was a normal part of living that everyone else had also inherited. I was unaware that the inheritance of genes within human bodies is different among different blood lines. I never thought to look outside of my own immediate family for an evaluation as to whether or not how I felt was normal. In this comparison with family members, I deemed that what I was enduring was at least somewhat normal.

As the decades began to pass, I noticed that my health was worsening, not to the point of being totally dysfunctional, but definitely progressing into a more unsustainable existence.

After a long trail with an assortment of doctors over the decades, none of them seemed to be able to hit a definitive diagnosis. When I turned fifty years old, I finally landed at an extraordinary cardiologist's office. I would see for the first time someone who would exhibit a determination to uncover the true identity of the culprit in my health problems.

On the day of my first exam with my new cardiologist, he walked into the examination room, looked at me, and asked if anyone had ever mentioned Marfan syndrome to me. I responded to his question immediately and informed him that I had another family member that very week at the genetics department at a local hospital clinic being evaluated for just such a syndrome. With his instructions, a few weeks later I followed up with the same genetics department where my other family member was being diagnosed with Marfan syndrome.

Marfan syndrome is an inherited disorder that affects connective tissue, the fibers that support and anchor your organs and other structures within your body. This syndrome most commonly affects the heart, eyes, blood vessels, and skeleton. The most serious complications involve the heart and aorta with an increased risk of mitral valve prolapse and aortic aneurysm.

On the day of my appointment, I was clinically diagnosed with Marfan and Ehlers-Danlos syndromes. In recent years, several other family members have gone to the same clinic, where they too were evaluated for these syndromes and have been diagnosed with one or the other. I am the only one scoring on both syndromes.

At my cardiologist's office during my next evaluation, we discovered that I have had multiple heart defects due to this genetic defect. This appears to be the culprit for my lifetime of fatigue, among other symptoms. In light of my family history, I was also advised by my cardiologist and genetics doctor to have genetic testing done for genetic breast cancer, having had so many cases of this disease throughout my family, including my mother and sister.

I resisted the notion that I would have yet another genetic disorder, so I continued to decline this request by both doctors; that is, until I had a few years to comprehend and adjust to the knowledge of the connective tissue disorders.

Finally, with my doctor's prompting, I agreed to the genetic testing for breast cancer, and with the blood drawn and sent for testing, I waited. I waited, anticipating that this would finally put to rest any future speculations of my developing the same cancer that plagued some other members of my family.

My wishful thinking was actually what was put to rest on that rainy morning when I arrived at the clinic and my doctor informed me that my test had come back positive for the BRCA-1 gene. With this news, my thoughts and my world came to a screeching halt. I knew the implications of this gene being present in my DNA, but still I walked away with denial in my heart that this mutated gene would actually cause me to develop the cancer. Earlier in my life, I had seen this cancer manifest in the lives of many other family members, never ever conceiving that this would be the future reality for my own life.

A few years passed, and I adjusted to my connected tissue diagnoses and the changes that were now being implemented to make life easier and safer for me. Then the thoughts of preventive surgery to avoid the breast cancer became a consideration. This thought was only a consideration because of the risks involved in having surgeries while enduring my current health deficits. Since I had heart defects and a history of extreme allergic reactions to drugs, any surgeries would be considered high risk. Weighing the pros and cons became a preoccupation with no clear resolution.

By August 2012, considering surgery was no longer an option. A mysterious lump had appeared in my right breast, and I was diagnosed with breast cancer. The surgery was no longer an option. It was now a necessity.

The new challenge at hand for my doctors was to earn my cooperation. I had become a person wretched in fear of even approaching this world of surgeries and treatments. At this point I had accumulated entirely too much negative information in my head.

After several failed attempts to find a skilled team willing to accept my situation, the challenge was met head-on by the University of Virginia. At last, I entered the world of surgeries and treatments dictated by my cancer diagnosis. Despite my overwhelming fears, I started the surgeries and treatments in April 2013.

As any person fighting cancer can attest, this battle can be difficult at times, to say the least, but we must move forward despite mental and physical challenges. This team saw past the fear and was able to reduce my fearful state of mind. Thus, we were able to move forward and fight the cancer.

My cancer turned out to be very difficult. It was termed the worst-case scenario in every category. With many battles, I continued with radiation and chemotherapy treatments after the surgeries, none of which seemed hopeful for a cure or remission of my cancer. Finally, after four different chemo treatments either not working or being intolerable, I alone decided to not pursue any further chemo treatment. The cancer is currently in my lungs, chest wall, bones, and lymph nodes. The chemo at this point would have little, if any, pain relieving effect for my remaining life. My decision was to finish out my life as peacefully as I could.

Given three months or so to live back in October 2014, I feel very blessed to still be alive writing and living my life with reasonable restrictions.

The takeaway of my story is this: everyone must take the history of their family seriously and research and seek medical advice for what is available for your particular risk. Also, try hard not to let any fears hold you back when the scary procedures become necessary. Time lost to fear can be time the cancer uses to advance.

I don't know what chance I ever had with the worst possible breast cancer within me, but I did learn to live to the best of my abilities through this process with all of the tough decisions that had to be made. Right or wrong, they were mine to make, and I will now live out my fate with no regrets. Decisions made can't be revisited or changed anyway. And who's to say with any certainty that any different decisions would have changed the outcome?

The PET Scan

I just want something to eat, is that asking too much? Obviously it is, because I've been given orders NPO, which mean nothing for the patient orally, and for this procedure that means at least six hours prior to check in. Well, I just hit my six hours, and it feels more like a day and a half. So my starvation continues as I wait.

As I sit in the waiting area with many other patients seated all around me awaiting the same or similar procedures, I wonder what might be the story each would tell if any of us were brave enough to strike up a conversation. Going through the cancer center, I have come to realize that there is a common thread in our solitude while waiting on our procedures. Most often when eye contact is made, it's accompanied by a counterfeit smile, and it's usually quickly disengaged. There are some exceptions, but all too often this is the pattern of avoidance.

I can usually find logic in a lot of human behavior, but for this one I'm not really sure. What are we afraid of that causes such a disconnection with so many? I wish we could open that curtain, because the people I have had the privilege to meet in the cancer centers have been a treasure to me in this trying time. I just wish we were more social in the cancer center setting.

I experience mixed emotions as each name is called and another person disappears behind a door. All I want is to get my procedure of the day over with, yet I want to draw out every moment till my name is called, dreading what lies ahead of me. Deep breath taken, I continue my wait, which seems longer than usual today, only adding to my agony.

With the standard, "How are you today?" Mike, my tech, leads me back to the usual beige recliner chair to receive the dreaded IV. I am a bit problematic because my veins are almost nonexistent, and true to form, Mike is unable to find a vein. Enter Derrick. Fortunately, the second tech is successful, and the nuclear tracer is administered. Great, now I will *soak* for ninety minutes before I'm placed in the PET scan machine. Soaking, as it is called, is the time during which I wait for the tracer to spread throughout my body to the point it is even in my bones. Yikes!

Every three months, I am scanned, and with each scan I am told the cancer is progressing. I hold out hope that with this scan, I could, for once, get some good news. I'll spend my ninety minutes soaking and watching whatever is on HGTV, then I'll enter the scanning tube and get this over with.

After leaving the PET scan and the cancer center behind, my husband and I venture across the road to the hospital lobby for a late lunch. He parks me and our roll-around luggage loaded with food, and I wait in the nice seating area in the hospital lobby while he goes for the famous hospital cafeteria french fries. When he returns, hot fries in hand, we enjoy our lunch together. Then I am able to finally balance my blood sugar, which allows me to once again regain control of the English language that I have been blotching for the last hour or so. When my blood sugar falls too low, I don't speak words properly, and I always welcome having that little problem corrected.

After we eat our meal, we leave the hospital once again, completing one of many trips made over the last two-plus years. The test behind me, and well-fed, we make the hour-long trip back home. Home is the place where I am always trying to return these days—that place of comfort with no needles, undesirable tests, test results, or treatments. Home—where even though it can get a bit boring at times, it is always safe.

All is finished for this day, and I can rest. I know these tests are a necessity for the rest of my life. I just resist them and long for normalcy. I will see what tomorrow brings as I patiently wait for the results of today's testing, hoping to break the cycle of bad news. Living a life of uncertainty takes some adjustments in my thinking, and I pray for strength while learning these adjustments. All any of us can do is the best that we can and try not to come up short of all of our expectations.

"I will catch you when you fall," he said. "Then catch me," she said.

Why Norma Writes

I write at this stage of my life mostly because my life is dwindling. You see, my mind hit a whole new level of awakening and awareness with the diagnosis of terminal cancer. I had heard those words that we all, deep down inside, fear to hear coming from the doctor sitting across from us. Everything I ever did or planned to do became distorted and blurred. In that moment, right was wrong, up was down, and I found myself seemingly walking on a sea of memory foam in the solitude of my mind as I returned to my car.

Who was I supposed call, and then what would I say? How would I hold myself together to convey this news? On the day of my initial diagnosis, I was alone physically and mentally. It felt as if my mind decided to meditate on the information and leave the existence of the rest of me out of it. My thoughts became sloppy, and I slowed down to allow my mind to catch up as I drove home.

I drove into the same garage and entered through the same doorway, but somehow it all seemed foreign. My thoughts where elusive and at rest in my mind, refusing to accept the information given to it by my doctor. When would this fog I was walking in lift and allow me to take in the diagnosis I had just been given?

The phone calls were coming in to check on my doctor's visit, and all I was inclined to do was give a slow-motion glance at my phone. After a moment had passed, true to form, I took a deep breath and started to call the people closest to me. My competence was at last returning. The valve in my mind that was holding back the steam of my frustrations and fears loosened, allowing me to see with more clarity and a rational mind.

How will I approach this situation that I have been launched into? I'll tell you how: with the same strength and determination that I have possessed throughout my life. This cancer is the fear everyone sidesteps until they're confronted with it. Now I must confront that fear with all the dignity, strength, hope, and faith that is within me.

I am forced to accept this diagnosis for the time being, but I will not embrace it. It is unwelcomed, and I intend to let it know that by any means available to me. I know my battle will be exceptional due to existing health problems, but still, here I go on this trial, as difficult as it may be, where I will learn as I go and pray to make right decisions.

I have often prayed to God to use me in this journey of life, to help bless the lives of those around me who are in need. Maybe at this moment in my life, I am standing exactly where I am supposed to be. Maybe, just maybe, I will be strong enough to help those around me in this same battle to find some comfort. I will fight to survive and grow in my relationship with Jesus as I search for his wisdom to guide me.

I hope the words I write will both be enjoyed and endure. These thoughts will remain past my existence for those who understand them. Perhaps my words will fill a need and provide comfort.

So, write I will, even with the inconsistent feelings I'm experiencing, and I will share all the honesty, humor, love, and faith, and even fear that I have within me. May these words bring an understanding for whoever will cross my path with a willingness to hear my voice.

Most decisions we make have the potential to be right and wrong.
If we don't solve the wrong when implementing what we think is right,
then the right isn't as absolute as we think it is,
thus qualifying a reconsideration concerning the decision.

Ethel

I begin writing today with the deepest of respect for my well-loved grandmother, Ethel. I was not with my grandmother the day she passed away, but the story of that day and that moment was conveyed to me and has left an imprint upon my heart all these years. My grandmother and I had three counties between us. Coupled with my struggle to raise three small children, this meant I was unable to spend the amount of time with her that I desired, even when she became very ill. All I had to offer her, unfortunately, was one visit in that brief time while she was dying. Fortunately for my grandmother, our family was very large, and she never experienced a moment alone at the end of her life. This is the story that has endured time—the story of the things I know and the things conveyed to me pertaining to my grandmother and the day she found her peace. I can only hope that my humble interpretation does this special lady justice.

This story begins with the members of my family who were fortunate enough to be gathered around my grandmother Ethel's bed on the day she died. You see, Ethel and her husband Eddie had eighteen children, which netted them many grandchildren. I cannot even speculate on the correct number, so for the sake of moving forward with this story, we will just stick with *many*.

My widowed grandmother, whom I have always loved and respected, was slipping away from us, as her heart was now failing at the age of eighty. The fluid that was being retained in her body had changed her appearance as we had known her, but somehow the essence of who she was still shined through. Even in her present vulnerability, we could still sense the strength that had carried her and her family through all that life had thrown her way.

It was increasingly evident for those who were present that Ethel was now living in her final moments. Silence sometimes filled the air, as no one seemed willing or able to express the feelings that danced around their minds.

Many cherished friends and family had filtered in and out of the bedroom and stood at Ethel's bedside to offer their hand to hold hers. They offered a rub on her arm and an occasional kiss to her cheek or forehead. There was, at times, much talk of fond memories and admiration for this adored woman. A woman who, by the side of her husband Eddie, had not only successfully raised eighteen children, but had done so it in the toughest of times, during the Great Depression. I was, and am still proud, to call her my grandmother.

I could still feel her love for me deep inside even though I was not present during those final moments. I somehow felt her love even at a distance as she passed from this life and from her story. There remain many stories of Eddie and his bride, how they struggled with poverty as sharecroppers, and how together they shared their love with so many.

With tear-filled eyes, those with her saw the beauty in Ethel's departure from this world with the apparent return of her Eddie that day. If for only a moment, Ethel saw the face of her beloved husband once more while she still remained in her mortal body, for he had appeared to her. Before her last breath, Ethel found the strength to once again rise up a bit in her bed to acknowledge the man whom she now saw standing at the foot of her bed. With a childlike innocence, she pointed to Eddie and called out his name. It was to Ethel as if the time that had stood between her and her Eddie for so many years since his passing away had now disappeared. Had she returned to a time so long ago with Eddie, or was he now returning to her in the present time? She reached out to what she envisioned as the spirit of the man she had loved and only she could see. It was said that, in that moment, it appeared that nothing or no one in that room existed in Ethel's sight but the image of her Eddie. Only she could see Eddie because she could see him through the eyes of her spirit. The depth of the love they had shared was realized in that brief moment. Then Ethel released her last breath to leave those of us left behind on Earth and join her Eddie once again for eternity.

That day, I gained a better understanding of life and God's love. Without her powerful love for Eddie and his for her, my grandmother would not have had the last second of her life enthralled in the presence of *their* everlasting love.

She is no longer here with us, but her story will continue from generation to generation in all of us who are left behind. I know

now that my grandmother is in the peace and love that God has promised to us all. God had, in that moment of passing, allowed her and Eddie to glimpse that love in its vastness. I believe in my mind and in my heart that my grandparents are now dwelling together in a spiritual love that *is* the love of God.

The Gift Shop at Nag's Head

"When was the last time we were in Nag's Head?" I asked as we unpacked our suitcases for the weekend in the motel. I think we skipped last year, so that would make it two years since our last trip. After lunch we both felt like taking a nap to recoup the energy lost from the long trip we had just made.

Naps are short at our mature age, so no more than a few winks later we were up and ready to venture out. Feeling refreshed we decided to go and nose around . . . Oh, who am I kidding? We wanted to shop in The Farmer's Daughter shop like it was Christmas. The weather was beautiful, mocking the youngsters we used to be, we opted to walk hand in hand to the shop instead of driving. After all, it was only one lot away—an achievable journey for us both.

The atmosphere was amazing, and our little walk was refreshing and rewarding on such a splendid day. We arrived through the double front doors of the Outer Banks gift shop and felt the familiar thrill that we had experienced in previous years. There's nothing like it in our neck of the woods. It seemed as if everything shimmered and shined and smelled good, and it felt like everything was highly necessary for the continuation of our life back home.

We lost all track of time, along with a fair piece of our money, and thought at this late hour it was best to venture back to the motel. I must admit I felt just a tad bit guilty carrying the bags filled with what were overpriced items. I felt the guilt just for a moment because, after all, it was vacation, and money was meant for spending on vacation.

Okaaaay!! What had happened to the weather wizards of the Outer Banks while we were shopping? Were we being punished for spending enough money on sparkly knick-knacks to put 2.5 kids through college? It was November, and the sky was about to burst with rain and the lightning and thunder had already arrived. Standing outside the doors of the gift shop (as the doors were being locked) we realized that we were faced with a dilemma.

We were both wincing at the reality of what we both knew was the only option . . . RUN. Now even though we were only one lot away, it seemed as if with the lightning striking and the thunder over-exaggerating every strike, we were miles away. With a defective heart, I was not a runner any more. In fact, I hadn't run since I was about twelve years old. I'm comfortable with being a walker. Well, that life choice had come back to bite me in the behind at this moment. No time to second guess this, we must attempt running and right now before our situation becomes even more dire.

Hand in hand, we set our sight on the motel only a short distance away and started to run—if that's what you want to call it. It was actually kind of a gallop or fast walk until the lightning struck about halfway there along with a sudden downpour. Then that little twelve-year-old girl returned to me, and my run was on. Not just any ole run, but a run of utter fear. I may have enjoyed finally running after all these years had it not been for the fear of being struck by lightning or having a heart attack. Those thoughts took all the fun out of this childhood joy.

We did it. We made it to the safety of the balcony cover. Rick was unlocking the door to our room when I decided to raise the camera that was hanging around my neck and preserve the moment by taking a picture of him with the raging storm in the background. As I turned my attention and the camera towards the heart of the storm, the shutter clicked just as the lightning flashed—and the photo of the decade was taken. I knew the strike of lightning was in that shot, and indeed it turned out to be in there when the photos were developed.

That day caught in the unseasonal thunderstorm was embedded in our minds forever, and preserved as well on the impromptu photo. Lesson learned: never trust the Outer Banks weather Wizards.

*My mind, as I am dying, is mimicking that of
the supernova when the large star is dying.
I cannot contain all that is trying to escape
from within this gray matter.*

Peace

Sometimes the prospect of death reminds us where we have been and where we are in our own journey of life—a journey that has catacombs with twists and turns of decisions, and we are the navigators.

Perhaps there is something more. Is there a power greater than ourselves? Greater than destiny? A power with purpose and a desire for us? Let us be reminded of the purpose of life, the only purpose that makes sense of our existence here on this planet. I believe in a discovery that is to be made by us all. That discovery is in a creator that is alive and more powerful than the universe.

Our destiny playing out before us should be explicit, and we should be discerning enough to recognize that we should come to know the God of our creation. What a fulfilling proclamation: that we are here to accept the truth revealed to us of the creator and father of all humanity. This knowledge is the truth that joins us all together as one family.

Would our acceptance of this God of ours satisfy our hunger for the truth of our existence? I can say that I have tasted the word of truth in the Holy Bible, and my hunger was satisfied. My peace in understanding was finally found within my very soul. This was my test, my time to learn, my time to accept or deny. I chose to accept the word of truth and love. Anything short of Gods' love and the sacrifice of Jesus would not give relevance to my existence. We are not just an evolution of a bacteria. We are intelligent enough to have the longing for the truth. Deep down inside, we all know there is more to this life we are given on Earth.

When do we decide to slow down and search our soul and open our minds to the truth of where our spirit is longing to be? Faith is the reality of our acceptance—faith that will reside in the love that was promised to all who come to him through Christ Jesus, that we may live eternally in that love that is our God. I am satisfied that I am forgiven and destined to be with my savior in the kingdom from which everything exists. Old things will become new as the Bible says, and I believe that for my spirit. I am washed clean and forgiven.

There's a peace that comes to me as I understand that I will reside in Heaven with my Lord. It is a peace that defies understanding and beckons to be felt within the persons who possess that understanding.

The Little Kids

I was under the impression that when I arrived at adulthood, my growing was over. Well, clearly that only applies to physical growth. Despite the education offered at various levels of school and the best attempts of our parents to ready us for the world, when we reach adulthood, we find that much more learning still lies ahead.

I grew and learned a lot in my life while raising my children, and also later with my involvement in my grandchildren's lives. The biggest lesson I have learned over these wonderful years is that, if we allow the talents possessed by these children to be expressed, we can also discover some of those same talents hidden inside ourselves. We can then continue to grow in an undiscovered area with the children now before us. Even if the interest or talent does not exist within us, we should recognize these interests in the children and allow them to grow from the inside out, never limiting their experience to our own expectations. Of course, we must protect and council them to avoid things that are harmful or evil.

We should allow them to taste the world of childhood exploration around them, then we should be open and observe their reactions and determine their true talents and interests. Fortunate is the child who has parents who guide and allow them to discover and experience the many good things in their world. That is the child who can develop into their full potential.

Are our miracles sometimes so unique that we at times do not recognize them as such?

In the Mind of This Writer

When I write, it is as if there is a party of stories going on in my head and words are the confetti. I have a thought, and then the words find their way into my developing story. They always seem to fall in place *just right* to describe what it is that I'm feeling. It's amazing that they are all around me waiting to be harnessed, like catching beautiful butterflies with a net from a massive, endless swarm. There is a quest within my mind that never fails to satisfy my imagination. I am grateful for the ability to express that imagination, along with my life stories as well.

Writing is a friend who is there for me even on the darkest of days. Sometimes the momentum to write seems to go away, and I am left to wonder where all the ideas and words are hiding. Then they return to me, and I see that they were never really gone at all, just taking a rest deep in my mind. I awaken, alas, in that place in my thoughts where they are ready once again to come together in my mind to form something intriguing.

Do I dare to set these words of my mind's conjuring free; and if I do, will I be confining them to remain on the paper where they may eternally rest? They are just biding time till their true freedom is realized in the memory of those who read them. As long as the books exist, the words will persist as an immortality of stories.

Writing for me is a world within a world—stories with an atmosphere of words to bring them to life, an escape to all who venture to read them. As a matter of one's own opinion whether it be for better or for worse, they now exist on these pages, defying time to remain behind long after I am gone. How many more ways can I explain how I feel about writing? I'm a writer. I could go on for the rest of the day and still have open options for explaining my passion.

Collect all the words together to form a story, then collect the stories to form a manuscript. Present the manuscript to a publisher, and when accepted, it becomes a book for all to experience. What a blessing the arrival of my first book has been. So in my life now, by the validity of these accumulated words, I am humbly transformed . . . I am an author.

How Long till Midnight?

I glance once again at the clock across my bedroom perched on top of my chest of drawers. It is placed, by necessity, next to my TV. 11:30. I'm still awake. I continue to lie in the darkness with my light having been clapped off with the assistance of the clapper plugged in next to my bed. Cancer, surgery, and radiation have damaged my chest, so it has become too painful for me to reach the light sitting on my nightstand. I found that a clap was less stressful on my body than twisting and stretching for the light switch. What was perceived as silly many years ago when the commercials first came out has now become a well-appreciated and necessary item.

Lying in the darkness I find myself focusing on the reasons behind the somewhat tolerable pain in the left side of my chest (the cancer). While the pain is not great it is strong enough to hold my attention and keep me awake.

I have learned this lesson: that if we are to exhibit any level of intelligence in practicing our self-control then we must achieve the ability to redirect our focus to something more conducive to relaxation, so we can fall asleep.

I reposition myself in my bed in search of a more comfortable position to ease the pain. My thoughts are currently on how it felt to hear the words no cancer patient wants to hear— "metastatic." This word of resistance turned my fight against cancer into a lifelong and relentless fight.

Finally, I achieve what I perceive to be the best position for total body comfort, then attempt to find a more pleasurable subject on which to focus my thoughts. I'm still awake.

Within seconds, my mind takes me to the day Cloverleaf Mall opened in Chesterfield County back in 1972. Why I'm here in my thoughts I do not know, but these thoughts should do the trick. Having already said my prayers, I allow my thoughts to wander back to a time and event that I remember fondly.

My body has become one with the memory foam mattress, and my thoughts are where I can feel the tension releasing in target areas on my body. I am pleased at this moment to be where I am in my thoughts, considering my physical and emotional state. You see, by taking myself back to these innocent memories, not only do I enjoy reliving that event in my life, but I also gain a greatly needed appreciation for the privilege to have had this life to live, as imperfect as it is. I find that when I redirect my thoughts to the pleasurable moments, that is one more small victory over all the negative, hurtful, and frightening times that were and are a part of my life. Only in these moments of pleasant thoughts are the undesirable thoughts put to rest somewhere further back in my mind and out of sight. And if they try to return during this practice of relaxation, I will chase them back to where I had previously sent them. I alone possess the control as to whether I remain on the bothersome thoughts or change them in favor of thoughts that can bring a smile to my face.

So now I lie here in my bed in the darkness, with a smile that no one can see except God. I continue down the corridor I am entering in a mall that in reality no longer exists.

Cloverleaf Mall was torn down in 2011 to make way for a new shopping community more accommodating to the needs of the present-day shopper. However, in my mind tonight, it is still fully erected in all its splendor. I still remember so many places within its boundaries, from the candy, clothing, and music stores, to the big anchor stores on the end of each corridor, to the fountain worthy of complementing the grandeur of the mall that resides in the center of its crossroads. It draws both young and old alike with their pennies in hand, ready to toss them into the splattering water of the fountain. Each holds out hopes that their wishes made may come true.

I remember visiting each and every store with friends and family, and can even still remember some of the purchases I made over the years. A brand-new pair of blue jeans for $6.00!

With only one eye open, I take a quick glance again at the clock and become aware that it is now 11:47. Still awake. So as not to dwell on the present time or my goal to be asleep before midnight, I resolve to continue my stroll down memory lane in that mall of yesteryear.

I remember walking around the mall with a friend, making a spectacle of ourselves by creating a ruckus with our honking on the free kazoos given out to the shoppers that day. I don't think the promoters considered just how obnoxious, attention-seeking teenagers could be with this free token. I don't believe in my lifetime I've ever seen this item given out to the masses again. We were actually asked to leave one of the anchor stores because of all the disruption we created. I would not have thought that this bad behavior in my youth would decades later turn out to net great dividends in my life by assisting in relieving some of my suffering. Lesson learned: don't beat yourself up for some of the harmless stupid things you did as a kid. They may come back to you one day when you need them most and put a smile on your face.

Morning arrives, and I had one of my better night's sleep. I was unaware when I fell asleep. I just drifted into sleep in the memories of the old Cloverleaf Mall. I also never saw 12:00 on that tattletale clock, so I gained a bit more confidence in my ability to change where my mind plays at night. Peaceful thoughts can pacify instead of doing battle in the mind, and this can be restorative to my soul and contribute to my healing both physically and mentally.

Your spirit, your thoughts, your brain, and then your body, but where is your spirit? That is where it begins. I have a gentle spirit because it stays on Christ, who is of God the father, who is love. And many nights, my mind walks with Christ on His journeys, which I have read in the Bible.

There are so many beautiful thoughts to be explored within our minds. I have found that the more I fight back the bad thoughts and allow myself to enjoy the retrievable, kinder thoughts, the easier it becomes to stay within more pleasurable boundaries. It does take some effort, but I don't dread the nights. I take command of them.

As I hear the crow somewhere in the woods,
he tells all he has seen with such an unruly racket.

The Field of Entertainment

An old oak tree still stands in the open field across the road from my house. This is the field that all too often is my entertainment as I sit alone, not feeling well. This trunk of a tree is still a giant, standing about twenty feet high. On this day, I am watching a beautiful hawk end its flight across the field. He perches on top of the decaying tree, his wings expanding and then folding against his body. I can only speculate why he does this. Perhaps he is considering the prey below him in the field and is readying himself to attack, then reconsidering his chances. Or perhaps it is as I was once told by a wise man: that these birds are simply cooling themselves down with this activity. Only the hawk knows what he is seeing through his eyes at that moment or what thoughts are going through his mind.

At last, the hawk swoops down in a majestic display of aeronautics to the ground below him, but with the far distance between us, my eyesight will not reveal whether or not his hunt was successful. He ascends from the ground and out of my limited range of sight, and with the disappearance of the hawk, my entertainment must now be found in another source. My eyes now scan the distant field as well as my own yard for anything that may be scurrying about.

The hawk's disappearance was only momentary, for I can see his shadow moving around and about just outside my window on our freshly mowed lawn. His height in the sky conceals him from my sight, but the unescapable shadow charts his flight pattern on the ground. Entertainment once again returns to my sight and mind.

Soon, the shadow also disappears as he leaves for other hunting grounds. This innocent routine of a single hawk on this midafternoon brings some level of enjoyment to a lonely person, and he is unaware of his contribution. That thought only adds to the beauty of the moment.

With the departure of the hawk, I am not to be denied nature's entertainment, for now the field has produced a young deer to graze at the wood's edge—a deer young enough to still be sporting all its white spots. Slowly, it grazes with caution and offers me serenity on this day. He is another animal unaware of its contribution to the bigger picture of the life we all live together on this planet.

Little blessings can sometimes mean so much more than what they appear to mean. I enjoy that thought as I witness a sudden gentle summer shower chase the youthful deer into the woods. The scene changes again as I now focus on the raindrops in the dried-up and deserted birdbath just outside my window. I know that when the birdbath fills with rainwater, it will provide new entertainment later as the local birds come. Baths will be taken, and thirsts will be quenched as I secretly watch them.

I humble myself these days to these enjoyments outside my window. They have now become my preference as my TV sits idly in front of me, waiting to be viewed only when the cover of darkness conceals the activities outside. I find an enhanced peacefulness in watching nature, and that becomes pretty much the only benefit of being sick and so often trapped at home. It is most unfortunate to be so sick, but it does allow me to slow down and see things in a more appreciative way.

The silent simplicity of nature reveals God's intent of how life for us was meant to be, but somehow we take a few wrong turns and often miss the sweetness in these things. The hummingbird just retrieved his necessary pollen from my red geranium. Once again, I am grateful for this simple moment that passes by me as quickly as the breeze that brought the rain shower.

These little moments collectively weave a contentment within me that I will carry throughout the evening. They are simple little memories, but fulfilling when I am forced into this boredom. I am grateful to be enlightened enough to recognize that when life suddenly changes for us, we must adjust to those changes and find peace within their boundaries.

At last, the evening approaches and gives way to the creatures of the night, and even the groundhog has made his way across the yard to disappear into the woods. I will close my blinds and allow those creatures to remain in the privacy that the darkness allows them, and I will now share this evening with my husband living within the confinement of the time allotted us.

And Yet

The sun sets and the sun rises; and yet, I remain standing another day.

The clouds in the sky are so far away; and yet, my eyes see them in an instant.

A loved one takes their last breath and dies; and yet, at the same time, with its first breath, a child is born.

Lies are spread throughout the land; and yet, if only we would look, the truth is evident right before us.

The taste of success is sweet; and yet, it falters without the love of truth and honesty.

Sometimes we find that we will enter in one door; and yet, sometimes we must exit by way of another.

Strife may sometimes enter into our lives; and yet, we can still find resolve and retrieve our peace once again.

We can seek encouragement and find a void; and yet, contentment is standing there beside us.

Time seems to pass far too quickly; and yet, it seems to stand still in our memories.

A restless night can cause us concern; and yet, with the morning sun, there dwells a new hope.

Starvation deprives the world of precious life; and yet, we faithfully step forward to feed the hungry.

Our self-pride sometimes rises up to fearful heights; and yet, our humility can guide us to a more respectful existence.

Trials appear that seem to weaken our will; and yet, our strength can unmistakably prevail.

Fatigue will try to cease our momentum;
and yet, we rise to our feet once again.
Love may appear to be slipping away;
and yet, it can always be resurrected.
Sometimes our minds are stagnant;
and yet, with time, the words seem to always return.

Making a Sound

If a tree falls in the woods and no one is around to hear it, does it still make a sound? Really, do we ask this? Maybe the tree will not be remembered for the experience of losing its life alone in the woods that day, but its appearance on the ground testifies to the event, and the event would or could not exist without the sound. If I cry out for someone the day I die because I am alone, that solitude would not make my plea nonexistent, just the plea's resolve unsatisfied. We are all given an allotted amount of time to live when we are born, and death will not be cheated of its destiny regardless of what is heard or not at that moment. Tree or human, at the time of loss the sound and weather are irrelevant to the event happening. Just my humble opinion. And so, the question is put to rest in my mind.

Live

I want to live. It's all I've ever known. I don't know anything about dying, never done any of that before, although I did come pretty close a few times in my life. I'm surely not interested in trying it now—maybe in about another thirty years or so. It seems, however, that I have no choice in the matter, with each PET scan showing an increase in the cancer growth within my body.

I feel daily that my body is declining, and I'm unwilling to accept the truth of what is happening to me, while still holding in reserve a resistance of this data, which is unfailing. Sustaining life is ingrained in us all. Letting that go does not compute, no matter how hard I try.

I have felt this moment in my life for most of my life. I cannot impress upon any listening ear how great an appreciation I felt for the simplest of things of this world and how much greater that awareness grows at this time in my life. It was as if I intuitively knew my life was going to end a bit short of my expectations. And now, with that perceived time having arrived, I am experiencing a natural resistance.

Live I will with what time is allotted me as I wrestle with the idea of leaving behind every piece of my life, except for my spirit. My home, my clothes, the things I created, my children and grandchildren, my friends, and my husband will all left behind for someone else to enjoy when I am gone. I have no choice in the matter. All that will be left of me will be only a memory, and I question how long that will last with some people.

I feel this is so difficult because no one in my personal life of my generation or under has left this life. I am the first. The first: I can't fathom the meaning of this. God alone knows the meaning of what is happening to me. I must simply learn to accept his will.

With chemo and radiation, my words are starting to escape me, but I will try to sum my thoughts up as crudely as they may present themselves. I learned in this life to survive even while in very difficult situations, and I learned this well. God gifted me with several skills that allowed me to carry forward no matter what I had to endure, and for that I am eternally grateful. Now that I am in this time in my life where the struggles should somewhat subside, I must die, so I can only conclude that I must now struggle to survive, and I must trust. Trust in the very belief that I carry in my heart. Trust in the belief that we carry on beyond this world in an eternity beyond description, and I have that trust. It's just hard to let go of a life I learned to hold on to so tightly. I developed this picturesque life of mine so even in an imperfect world, now only to depart from it. That seems so contradictory to life itself. But in all actuality, it is simply an accomplishment completed and a transition towards a new one soon to begin—a new existence that will shadow all that I ever knew in this life. All that is left for me to accomplish now is to one day learn to let go.

Miracles come in different sizes and shapes and at different times.
Like snowflakes, they are unique in some small or big way to each of us.

Why Is the Donkey Tied Up Under the Tree?

Rain, rain, rain—that's all it seems to do anymore. I'm on my way back home from the mountains and more medical testing, when once again my husband and I find ourselves traveling in yet another downpour. With little else to do on this long journey, I once again turn my attention to whatever may catch my eye on the side of the highway, hoping for some level of amusement.

At last, there it is—something unusual to provoke thought in this wondering mind. A donkey all by himself, tied to a tree. *Why is the donkey tied to that tree in the rain?* I silently thought. It's a muddy area not worthy of grazing, so what might the purpose be? Is he a runaway who needs to be held captive? Maybe he is but a holding spot until his owner can later retrieve him. I shudder to think that this is where the donkey would regularly reside.

As our SUV continues down the highway, heading closer to home with every mile we put behind us, we also move farther away from the donkey. In seeing this lowly creature unable to defend himself against the dreadful weather, I learned something about myself. I can see that I am compassionate concerning both man and beast. I know this because I want to return to where the donkey was and lead him away to a proper shelter. Perhaps those are not unusual conditions for a beast of this type, but I feel a need to nurture everything living, including a lowly donkey.

The List

As a cancer patient, I have seen and learned more about this world than I care to elaborate on today. However, I would like to compose this helpful list for all the people who don't understand what it is like to be this ill and so in need of the people in their lives. Whether we are young or old or somewhere in between, our needs can be great at times. It can become hurtful when you simply must ask for help with something you can't achieve for yourself, and all who are contacted have more important things to do. I personally will give up and allow the need to go unmet as the list continues to grow. You can trust me in this: if I go as far as to ask for your help, you can be assured it is truly needed.

I wonder how many times these things could be worked out if the person really wanted to help. I will say that the overwhelming majority of excuses given these days, I would not have even mentioned to someone who had a need of my help. I would have simply changed the thing blocking my availability to help, and helped the person in need.

So, barring real life situations that are unavoidable such as childbirth, court, marriage, death, etc. Here is the list of acceptable excuses:

1.

2.

3.

4.

5.

Conclusion: There are none.

Lately, I have found more clarity and learned many more things. Even at the end, there's more.

The Breath

I have learned that God breathed the breath of life into man. I know in my mind, soul, and heart that this is true. I feel this inside of me all of the time, but never more than today. I sit outside of the safety of my home that has protected me from the winter storm of the year. Where I currently live with my husband, when the snowfall measures a foot or more, depending where the drifts are, it is considered significant. But that was three days ago, and now the sun finally shines a magnificent warmth. Its brightness gives evidence to the temperature that radiates from it.

Finally, I have escaped from the confinement of this home—a home that I have grown to appreciate and depend on so often as my health has declined. My escape is short in distance, only to the deck on the back of our home, but it is a taste of sweet indulgence in the warmth of the sun. Even in its bad condition, it still provides a sanctuary from the cold wet snowy ground just below where I now sit.

I take in all that this moment has to offer. My body is feeling the sun's warmth and my diseased lungs are filling with the crisp, cool clean air that blows across my face. I feel with each breath the breath of life God has given to us all. The perfect sweet air I feel is all around me, the same as his love. The love and the clean life sustaining air that I breathe is of Him. I wish to remain in this awareness of His presence and the gift of His creation for as long as the warmth of the sun allows me.

Alas, only moments later, the heavy clouds return, and the coolness returns to what my frail body deems as an undesirable degree, so I must return once again inside our home for the warmth. I return inside with a renewed appreciation for our creator and the sustainer of life itself, Elohim (God our creator). And so once more, I am compelled to write about another thought, and this one was really to my liking.

Hot Sticky Feet on the Pavement

The lizard's color is green on the highway,
where he's seen with hot sticky feet on the pavement.
He goes for a run in the hot desert sun,
hot sticky feet on the pavement.
Many others join in and they're running with him,
hot sticky feet on the pavement.
Two more join the crowd and the group's getting loud,
hot sticky feet on the pavement.
They're all great friends and their fun never ends,
hot sticky feet on the pavement.
The water lies beyond a curve in a pond,
hot sticky feet on the pavement.
Climbing out the other side after cooling down their hides,
hot sticky feet on the pavement.
All the lizards pass a cat and a burrow with a hat,
hot sticky feet on the pavement.
They don't know where they're going
with the hot wind blowing,
hot sticky feet on the pavement.
The hill's so steep, winding upward with the sheep,
hot sticky feet on the pavement.
The lizards all slide down the other side,
hot sticky feet on the pavement.
Dust the dirt off their scales and the dust off their tails,
hot sticky feet on the pavement.
There are insects in the heat, so the lizards stop and eat,
hot sticky feet on the pavement.
The turtles are so slow, and they watch the lizards go with
hot sticky feet on the pavement.
The sign reads left in their sight, but the lizards go right,
hot sticky feet on the pavement.
They all missed their turn, and their feet still burn,
hot sticky feet on the pavement.

Not where they were bound, they wind up in town,
    hot sticky feet on the pavement.
Cars everywhere caused such a scare,
    hot sticky feet on the pavement.
The flashing traffic light gives them all a screaming fright,
    hot sticky feet on the pavement
They all turn around and head out of town,
    hot sticky feet on the pavement.
Running close together as the hawk drops a feather,
    hot sticky feet on the pavement.
His shadow drops low, and they don't know where to go,
    hot sticky feet on the pavement.
Hiding in the box nearby while the hawk's still in the sky,
    hot sticky feet on the pavement.
With the hawk now gone and the run's back on,
    hot sticky feet on the pavement.
As a car hits a bump and a bag falls out the trunk,
    hot sticky feet on the pavement.
It nearly hits them all, which makes them fall,
    hot sticky feet on the pavement.
Things not made for boys, they are little girl toys,
    hot sticky feet on the pavement.
Dolls everywhere with bows in their hair,
    hot sticky feet on the pavement.
The clothes look like new in lizard sizes, too,
    hot sticky feet on the pavement.
In just a while, they're dressed in style,
    hot sticky feet on the pavement.
With shoes on their feet, now they don't feel the heat,
    no more hot sticky feet on the pavement.

Now is alive, and so I am alive now.

Sins

If there is a line of humanity waiting for judgment, do I dare to think that my sins could be less than those who stand in front of me or those who stand behind me? Will my remorse be greater than those around me—or insufficient?

How much of the life I have lived will be judged as wrong, and how much of that wrong would I not have even recognized as sin? After all, it is apparently easier to see someone's sins than our own.

These thoughts cannot consume me, though they do appear within the boundaries of this human mind. For I do feel in my heart and in this human mind that I can present my confessions to Jesus Christ, then one day I can face my God washed clean of these sins, whether known by my consciousness or unknown. This is the truth that Jesus so often spoke of.

A teardrop descends down my face by the pull of gravity as I write. I can feel that the fear that dares to take root in my heart cannot even produce a spark. For I carry within me the flame of God's forgiveness as I am presented unto Him through His son Jesus. And all I had to do was listen, with not only my mind but also my heart, to the words of truth spoken by our savior Jesus Christ.

Truly, I will be humbled in His presence when that day of judgement comes. Then my trust in the judgment of Jesus is realized in that moment as the beautiful words of the Bible asked, "Oh death, where is your sting?"

My sins will be washed away by the blood of the lamb, and this is the reality I should understand and know now as I am living. I will fall to my knees and give thanks for the freedom I can experience, knowing this salvation while I am still within the human body.

I can see that whose sins are heavier is not the question, but rather who receives the forgiveness to lighten that load and loosen the grip upon us that evil attempted achieve. A decision that lies within us all to be made by the mind and the heart. I never found this decision to be a difficult one to make. Its simplicity and beauty make it a natural and fulfilling choice easily made and embraced by me. I am grateful for the gift of eternal life that is offered to us all.

Whispered Words

We have all had many moments where someone in our presence has moved us with their words. I can think of many: I love you, It's a girl, It's a boy, You're a very talented writer, You inspire me, to name a few. But one stands out and is deeper in my heart than any.

The gentle words that I hold so closely to my heart was in the whisper of a secret to my ear. Not just any secret, but that of a child. I have always been able to connect on an astonishing level with children, and this very young child honestly loved me. That day the love and our encounter were appreciated by us both.

I sat that day on the sofa in my living room with this precious child who was not yet even old enough for school. And as we were playing together with the other family members around us, the sweet child raised those little hands and cupped them around my ear. I listened attentively and heard that sweet voice say, "I wish we could stay here forever." I knew that by saying "we," this child's desire was for her parents and sibling(s) to also stay with her forever. How precious this was for me. I often think of this little whisper, and it always brings a smile to my face. In some of my roughest moments, this memory helps brighten my spirit.

I don't remember exactly my response. Only the echo of those words whispered to me remains in my memory. I don't know if there is a hug big enough to encircle this endearing secret entrusted to me.

And yes, sweet child, I also wish you all could stay with me forever.

*We are **all** going to come up short,*
miss the target, and get it wrong sometimes.
Make sure we learn from our mistakes
and don't succumb to repetitiveness.

What Is This Fight?

If this cancer wants my life, then it's going to have to fight for it. I am not the type of person to give up. I have to look at this as a challenge, and I am a very competitive person. Cancer comes deceitfully to steal my life, the dirty little thief that it is.

Traditional chemo and radiation treatments aren't always all that is involved in achieving success in fighting cancer. I will turn to my own tenacity and also to our God and Savior, who has a plan greater than these rogue, divisible cells. If this cancer developed in my life, then perhaps this was a trial that I was to endure, but where it goes from here and the duration of my life is still questionable.

In considering this cancer, I ask myself sometimes what may be the driving force that allows the continuation of my survival beyond what I was told by my doctors? There can be so many assumptions, and I believe they all accumulatively may be what sustains me. I will never underestimate all of the supportive people with prayers fighting along beside me. And as I *believe* in the will of God and trust in His timing, I am free to strive to achieve the goals that seem unachievable.

Miracles

Miracles come at different times in our lives and in different sizes and shapes like snowflakes. They are unique to each of us. Sometimes they are so minute that we do not even recognize them, or so enormous that we proclaim them to the world. However, they are not always present in our lives. Sometimes we are to endure trials, for trials do bear a purpose, whether we like them or not.

I have been blessed with many miracles in my life and recognize that if at some point the miracle doesn't come, it doesn't mean that I am forgotten by my LORD. Sometimes changes come about on this planet and in our lives that are not pleasant. That is when we are learning to move our faith to a higher level. Where is the need for testing our faith in pleasure? That level of testing within ourselves comes during these trials.

I have found my faith to be sound and my love for the LORD to be strong. This was achieved through my relationship with our living Savior Jesus Christ. I have never felt truly alone, even during those times when I was void of human companionship. I will be victorious in this trial, and one day stand before my Lord. Being victorious does not always stand up to the world's definition. It is instead defined by our Father, and in that we must trust. Do we hold on so strongly to this life that we don't even recognize miracles or purposes when they are right before us?

Learn and enjoy life. But always accept God's changes as they present, and never judge Him. Simply put trust in Him while in all situations that present in life.

July 20, 2016 10:00 am
Bad Timing

The contentment that I thought I could enjoy this morning has once again been cut short with the insatiable barking and howling from my new neighbor's young bird dog.

I walk outside to my front yard in the morning breeze that is unseasonably cool for late July. I sit in a folded chair that was placed tightly against the house under the roof of our small front porch, avoiding the rain of last night's thunderstorm. For the brief few minutes before the ongoing barking, I heard a familiar sound: the sound of the flock of geese returning to the small pond that lies on the far side of the field across from my house. Along with the geese announcing their arrival to our small neighborhood, there are the songs of many early morning birds. Not to be outdone are the cicadas making their transitional cries of summer.

The approximately five minutes of piece I am afforded is as sweet as a single swallow of water after being marooned in the desert for many days with no water. You see, now that I am dying, I feel more desire for the peace of nature that God has allowed us to enjoy. However, all that I came outside to meditate on has been compromised by the sheer volume of this dog's relentless barking. Once again, I'm retreating back inside my home.

I know my time to die is nigh, as last night I was coughing up blood. I reason that this can't be good. I have coughed from the cancer in my lungs for a long time now, but never produced blood like this before. Oh, I wish to return to the peace of nature I have enjoyed over the years—but now I'm more accepting of the idea that others' needs often come first. Just really bad timing for me.

Be this as it may, this morning I will continue to try to find a sweet spot where the summer air is not too hot and humid for my delicate lungs and hope the dog may be preoccupied. Then I can escape this disease long enough to commune with the beauty of nature as I am meant to enjoy it with what little time I have left.

An Opinion

I sometimes cry out, *why me?* Then I resolve the simple truth is, *why not me?* Am I not to think that I am the better person and not deserving of such a life as this cancer has imposed upon me? I don't think the cancer cells are subject to the personality of the person they invade. They will attack a body regardless of any perceptions the person may have of their own self-worth or the lack of.

I truly believe in the bigger picture beyond this life, so maybe this is where I am *supposed* to soon be heading. If I profess my belief that everything and everyone has a purpose, then I must also profess that our existence in itself can change to fulfill that purpose. What if my leaving this life at this time is not for the purpose of anyone or anything left behind, but instead is possibly happening because of where I am going? Maybe that is where I can reach the full potential in my purpose. Only God knows where and when our existence shall change, so perhaps we should relax and just trust in His will, even when it does not coincide with our own.

I fight that I might stay alive, but for what, or for whom? Is our desperation to survive so great that we sometimes do not believe what we see when we are dying? As for me, at times the answer to this question is a definitive *yes.* I believe that desperation is sometimes greater than recognition. This existence that I am forced to live with now is sometimes judged harshly by the presuming thoughts of others, so I push myself past my current abilities in order to prove my gallant efforts to stay alive, thus disbursing the myth of an unfounded accusation of people such as myself self-willing to be sick or dying. This is an incomprehensible thought in itself, but I have heard this proclamation made with my own ears and was stricken speechless to hear these words coming from another person's mouth. Much of my exhaustion comes from trying to prove the nay-sayers wrong and thus losing the rest needed for this challenge. There exists a number of healthier people who try to tell us what is going on inside our bodies and our heads while living with this terminal illness. I say, that is impossible. If I must repeat for impact, then I say again, that is impossible.

I am thankful for my psychologists who have supported me in every way to lend strength and assist in my understanding of what is happening with me with the progression of this disease. They are always assuring and helpful, never judgmental. I am also thankful for the minority of people in my life who understand the difficulties that come with this disease and who unconditionally support me.

Yes, no matter how difficult this challenge may have been and still continues to be, I desperately try to always hold on to my will, hope, dignity, and determination. And where I hold my strongest confidence is in my faith, and *that* I believe will never falter or fade. Where I am in this particular process is mine alone to proclaim. I have come to a reality that I will fight on my own terms and stop trying to live up to anyone's expectations, however remaining grateful for all those who support me regardless of where I am in this walk or however long it may take. I will not give up the fight until there is no more resource left for me, and even then, that decision will understandably be made by me, my medical team, and the will of God, not by anyone else.

The process of my dying is just slow enough to allow me to believe that this challenge in my life is simply a phase, and that, in given time, will somehow be corrected. Cancer seems to play these games with my head by sometimes throwing wonderful hints of hope at me, only to resume its progression without any constraints to respect how I might will this situation. When did I lose the control of my wellness and these renegade cells? That control was always there, waiting for the opportunity to present itself; for those cells' control was birthed within my body with the BRCA 1 cancer gene.

Until I take my last breath, I am a survivor, and I will ask that how I fight to survive be respected. After all, everyone makes decisions every day that succeed or fail, and navigating through cancer is no exception. Love and prayer will always go a lot further with this cancer patient than lofty or judgmental opinions. That's my opinion.

An Old Hound Dog

Living far away from *town*, as we call it, was not really something I aspired to do, but there I stood in a wooded neighborhood with ten other houses. Every house in that small neighborhood had multiple acres. Our lot alone could have had somewhere around fifteen to twenty houses on it if it were where I came from in the suburbs of Chesterfield County.

Suffering from reoccurring migraines, I found the quiet of country living conducive to the type of environment needed to endure the immense pain and suffering involved with my frequent headaches. That was our motive for moving so far from our home and our life as we had known it for so long.

Now, hunting season was something I didn't take into account when I moved so far away in search of my solitude. I was in search of serenity apart from the noise suburban life was teeming with. At the time of our moving, there had never been any hunters in my life, so everything to do with hunting was obscure to me. We soon learned that the neighborhood where we moved used to be part of a hunting club's domain. That first autumn in our country home was our first experience with hunting season, and it became obvious to us that hunting dogs were no respecters of the invisible survey boundaries of our properties. During that hunting season in our new home, we became as proficient in the activities entailed in the field of hunting as we could, including dog hunting.

There was at times a degree of annoyance that came with the private property recognition challenged hunting dogs. They seemed to also have no understanding of the evening curfew of our neighborhood. We had come to a social indifference with these hunting dogs but quickly realized that we were not in the suburbs anymore and needed to adjust to our new rural environment. This meant that reaching an understanding with our four-legged property visitors was part of our baptism into this new culture. In time, critter-tracking visits became a bit of a novelty to us.

Pondering those dogs and their freedom to roam allowed me to escape into the thoughts of a lifestyle previously unknown to me. The adjustment came swiftly to both my husband and I, and we were eager to learn all we could about the rural way of life, including the shenanigans of these hunting dogs.

It was an unusually warm Saturday afternoon, so I decided to take advantage of the warmth by cleaning out all the once-beautiful summer plants in our flower beds that had now become brown and lifeless. Pausing with a sigh, I reviewed in my mind a list of more enticing adventures I could be engaging in at that particular moment. But then I quickly convinced myself that this chore was more nurturing to my soul and well-being than the alternatives, so I continued with the task at hand.

I could hear the hunting dogs in their chorus of what some might refer to as barks, but we knew better now. These were not barks, but a symphony of communication and excitement between each of them and the hunters—communication used for millennia between them with no need for the smart technology we have these days. Heritage is the word that comes to mind for me, this kind of communication between man and beast has seemingly always been there and still survives today. We learned to understand this cooperation between the two of them and respect their traditions, and it paid off for us in a big way.

As I continued my work, or as I like to refer to it, therapy, I attentively listened to the hunting dogs' song slowly dissipate in the distance. I allowed my mind to wonder as to whether their mission in the woods that day would be successful. I thought for a moment about whether the mind of that animal could comprehend the disappointment of losing the chase. Lost in that thought and my work, I was suddenly startled by an aggressive rustle in the woods just behind where I was crouched down in the flowerbed. Hunting dogs were not the only critters in the woods, so now I had a bit of apprehension and was almost reluctant to investigate the sound I was hearing. Before I could act on any investigation, the source of the sound was revealed to me as a hunting dog dressed in a collar and the painted numbers 44 on his side. He approached me directly from the tree line. Number Forty-Four, as he would become known as, had slowed his run down quite a bit and approached me in a calm walk as if he knew me well.

With the dog pack now some distance away, I was confused as to why this dog had deviated from the rest. Yet here he stood, eye-to-eye with me in my crouched position. Naturally, I spoke to him carefully, as not to allow myself to have direct contact with him due to my growing allergies. He was receptive to my conversation with him, and we became fast friends.

A few moments later, I realized I must seek out the owner of this dog. I thought for a moment and decided to contact my neighbor who had contact with the hunting club nearby. She lived deep within the woods and was adjacent to the property where the hunters continued to hunt, so I was relatively sure she could help me with finding out who this dog belonged to. Within moments, I had a name and phone number in hand and could start my search for Number Forty-Four's rightful owner.

The name I had written down and now had before me to call was Robert Bishop, a person at that time unknown to me. My husband Rick offered Forty-Four a treat, which he gladly took while I dialed the number. A kind voice answered and identified herself as Robert Bishop's wife. She took my information after hearing my story about our encounter with the hunting dog that still remained by my side. Seemingly amused by my story and my request to keep the dog if he is a troublesome deviator from the pack, she assured me that she would talk to her husband when he arrived home from the hunt.

The hunt must have been nearing its end because it wasn't long before the call came in from the hunter. Mr. Bishop obtained our address and was pulling in our driveway within moments. When he arrived, we were still entertaining the hunting dog, hoping to keep him nearby us so we could reunite him once again with his owner. Mr. Bishop was a bit older than myself, with a kind face and demeanor, and he appeared to be well-pleased to retrieve his missing dog.

Mr. Bishop asked us to refer to him as Robert as we all introduced ourselves. He immediately identified the dog as one of his own, and I was happy with their reunion. Still I felt compelled to ask if he was satisfied with the dog's performance considering he had deviated from the hunt. I asked this in hopes that maybe we could keep this dog that seemed to have as much interest in us as we did in him.

We learned that this was one of Robert's best dogs and that he had not been known for this kind of behavior before. I then tried to reason with myself as to why this hunting dog was attracted to me in my flowerbed when he exited the woods that day. And what, if any, purpose would lie behind his unusual behavior.

Number Forty-Four was now caged in the back of Robert's truck, and we lost sight of them both as they rounded the bend at the end of our driveway. Thinking we had seen the last of Number Forty-Four and his kind owner, we retreated back into our home with the day's adventures now at their conclusion. We could not have been more wrong, because Robert and Rick and I had contact with each other many times over the next few years pertaining to wayward hunting dogs. We welcomed the adventures or misadventures of these dogs for many years to come.

We had become friends with Robert as sure as we had with Number Forty-Four that Saturday morning a few years back. We moved away three years after our initial contact to where we currently reside in Powhatan County. Ironically, we now live closer to where our friend lives with his wife, for he did not live near our former residence but only hunted there. They reside very close to where we currently live.

When I was taken ill in more recent years, Robert was one of the people who not only became more involved in my and Rick's life; he also has withstood the test of time that I have been enduring my illnesses. He has been one of the truest of friends with us to date. I think that on the day that Number Forty-Four entered our property and Robert in turn entered our life, that meeting must have been some indication that there was purpose in the dog's visit. Now that I am fighting what has been deemed a terminal cancer, I can finally see the purpose of that dog's deviation from the pack that day. I believe that dog came into our life on that day to bring Robert Bishop into our life.

You see, not only did Robert come into our life, but so did many in his church family. There have been friendships forged and prayers of support by many. The carolers that have entertained us from the cold sidewalk for the last three Christmases were from his church. We have enjoyed a fellowship from this pivotal man and his church family in a way that is nothing short of inspirational.

Do I believe in miracles? Yes, I do, for I know that every day I am afforded to be here in this life is a continuation of the miracle that has been granted to me. I believe that my God would use that designated dog that left his mission of hunting that day to make contact with me and bring with him a miracle in the friendship that began between my husband and me and Robert. The event of that day defied explanation at that time, but has found a clarity today that brings gratification to my husband and me. This is a friendship that has birthed so much joy and nurturing for me during these toughest of times. It is a friendship that has extended throughout our community—all brought about by a wayward hunting dog and his owner. Imagine that.

Cancer Support Contract

Date: _____
Named contract beneficiary: _____

    This contract, effective immediately, assures physical and emotional care to the above mentioned.

    Those signed below agree to the terms listed here in.

    I (we) will spend a minimum of six (6) hours on either Saturday or Sunday of the assigned weekend with the contract beneficiary. Spending the night or staying the entire weekend is optional and negotiable.

    Duties will entail helping out around the house, cooking, and sharing company with beneficiary during a meal. Also having supportive and reminiscent conversations. Occasionally, arts and craft projects may occur during contractual visit.

    Cards or meaningful items brought to beneficiary by the person(s) signed below may be used as minutes spent towards the assigned six (6) hours agreed to be spent with the beneficiary. Items value to time allotted to be determined by the beneficiary.

    If the signer of this contract is unable to fulfill their obligations on their designated weekend, then it is their responsibility to find a replacement to trade, pay, or barter with said replacement to inherit contractor's weekend.

    Schedule is as follows:

Date: Person (s):

_____   _____

_____   _____

_____   _____

_____   _____

_____   _____

_____   _____

_____   _____

_____   _____

_____   _____

All who sign and honor this contract will be considered a participant in the well-being of the beneficiary's final months, weeks, or days. Appreciation will be acknowledged by the beneficiary for all signers of this contract.

All minor assignees above must be cosigned by a parent.

Beneficiary reserves the right to hold the hand of the above listed contract signers, occasionally express a bit of loving emotion, and accept any dub over visits that may occur.

I, _____, agree to the contract above and signing below obligate my time to the beneficiary, _____, under these mentioned terms.

Date: _____ Signature: _____

Contract Participant

Date: _____ Signature: _____

Beneficiary

My Plea This Morning

Today, I'd like to talk about what it's like to try and deny the cancer that is in my body. Anyone without cancer cannot know how hard it is to try to push that thought out of your mind once the doctor has planted it there. When a woman learns she is pregnant, there is very little time that the baby inside of her isn't on her mind. Well, it's kind of the same thing when someone learns that cancer is inside their body; it's a thought not easily shaken. The difference is that the baby represents life and the cancer represents death, so the cancer patient is expected to keep her thoughts to herself as much as possible, while the awaited baby is celebrated in conversations and activities. Both are life changing, and both are accompanied by changes in our mind.

Try as we may, it is at times hard to portray a false image of where we really are in our walk through cancer. The reality of cancer all too often is expected to be minimized so as not to disturb society around us.

Most of the time, I am just looking down on my situation, trying to comply with what society expects of me, and that is to deny that this cancer exists and not let it be representative of me. While practicing these charades, the cancer's existence can appear somewhat distant to me.

I know it's real, but I can often deflect its reality just enough to forget about being sick for a while. Then those days come where I can't turn away from what is happening to me. A reality check ensues, even though it is met with resistance, and it bursts through into a place in my mind where it had previously been blocked. Today is one of those days. Where do I go with how I am feeling today? Do I simply internalize it, as I all too often must do, or will I share my despair? I think I have already answered my own question by writing this essay. Maybe I don't get the human response I so desire from the keyboard, but at least I am releasing these thoughts in some way this morning. There is some level of satisfaction in recording my thoughts permanently in this piece I write today. I will now move on knowing that no one was here to hear my plea and fulfill the understanding I so hunger for, but one day someone will at least know that I had these feelings on this day. And that is sustenance enough to get me through the rest of the day.

They say cats always land on their feet, and I believe this to be true. I tried this experiment many times as a child and realized that the cat apparently has a foolproof method to avoid back injuries. Like the sure footed cat, I will land on my feet as long as possible. And I will also be thankful for my constant non-discriminating companion . . . my keyboard.

The White Farmhouse

I pass by that old white farmhouse on the right side of the road every time we travel to the Blue Ridge Mountains for my medical care. I always get a pretty good look at this house because it's relatively close to the road, not far from my passenger window. It's been abandoned the entire time we have been taking this trip down Route 522. This house looks in no way to be one of wealth, but simply an average farmhouse where a modest family would have dwelled. Perhaps they were farmers from a time gone by.

Consistently, I connect with these old abandoned houses and feel an energy within them. However modest it may have been on the scheme of historical significance, it is still history. Life was lived in these old abandoned houses as well as in the ones that are preserved.

There is a pronounced sadness within my heart as I watch this and many other old houses slowly disintegrate. Boards are hanging down, windows are missing at the hands of scavengers, foliage is growing around it in an uncontrolled manner, steps are rotten and broken through. It is evident that the old house will soon be destroyed. I long to bring this house and others back to that glorious day when a family first moved in with high expectations of living their lives in this new and perfect dwelling.

I ask myself, how many times were spring flowers planted in the border of that old home in anticipation of Easter's arrival? Perhaps Easter eggs were hunted in the tall grasses that were left to grow to conceal the eggs. The family would perhaps have been returning from church services, maybe the children ran and searched for the brightly-colored eggs with woven baskets in hand, while the father looked on at them and the fields he had plowed just last week. I imagine a smile on his face as he lit his pipe and enjoyed being amused by the active children. Inside in her protective apron tied around her Sunday best dress, the mother took the ham out the oven for one last check before returning it for just a bit more cooking. She pulled back the sheer Pricilla curtains and smiled at the sight that lures her out on the long back porch to join in on the laughter and fun in the massive backyard.

These are the thoughts I feel as I pass by these old houses. A harmless fantasy of sorts, or perhaps simple but beautiful snapshots of lives lived. As our journey progresses down the road and away from this old farmhouse, my eyes stay trained on the landscapes and clearings in the woods for the next old abandoned house so that I might conjure once more a tale of who might have lived there in the past. I will always wonder how close to accuracy my conjuring of these possible life stories may be. I can sometimes almost feel the lifeblood of their rich history and a beckoning to not be forgotten. I'm sure families still tell tales that were birthed from within their walls, thus keeping their existence alive long after they are gone.

Relay Day

Saturday was quite a day. The long anticipated twelve-hour day of Relay for Life had arrived in my beloved Powhatan County, and I was scheduled to speak on stage for the event. However, I was not feeling well enough to perform on stage in the ninety-degree weather that morning. I was not to worry though, for I had my back-up. You see, all those around me knew of this event, and two people stepped forward to be my accomplices in an extended act that was to go far beyond just my speech.

Entering the scene on that hot Saturday morning were two of my granddaughters, sisters Casey and Riley. After their arrival on Friday evening and our having explored the idea of the extended surprise performance, we spent some time discussing all that we had imagined, and with that, the rehearsals began.

Casey was to read my speech, followed by Riley singing a song and inviting donations to Relay for Life. With the weather being so hot and Casey having some restrictions herself, the speech and song were both shortened by mutual agreement.

My husband, Casey, Riley, and I arrived at Powhatan Middle School for the event at about 5:00 and explained our intentions to the program manager, who appeared to be excited with what was soon to unfold on stage. At the appropriate time, my granddaughters both took the stage. Immediately, Casey took control of the moment. I'd had no idea she was so comfortable in front of a crowd and could have such confidence as to address them in the entertaining manner in which she did.

Casey owned the crowd, and in my opinion, she was deemed as a professional. As Casey wrapped up speaking to the crowd, it was becoming apparent that her sister Riley was about to take flight from the stage. Unlike her sister, who had plenty experience on the stage, Riley was now in retreat mode with a moderate case of stage fright.

Casey made the statement before the crowd that poor little Riley was chickening out, but she would not allow her sister to do so. My heart ached for this poor ten-year-old who was now taking a step or two away from the microphone. My husband and I started the crow's requests that older sister Casey accompany her in performing the song. Having the showmanship that she did, Casey announced that of course she would join her sister in singing the song. And sing that song they did. The crowd was elated with the performance at its end. Casey had bailed her sister out, and so Riley made it through her stage fright. Riley had overcome the stage fright, and they were both renowned in their own small way that day. The applause and whistles revealed the crowd's approval.

With the speech and song finished as planned and Riley now having gained her confidence, she stepped forward and announced that the dollar bill she held in her hand would be the straw that broke the camel's back in funding a cure for cancer. She threw the dollar forward off the stage into an empty trash pail we had brought from home. My husband and friends of ours threw in their dollars as well, and for the next five minutes, these girls raised $120.00 from the people who stepped forward to join the contribution of that dollar bill that broke the camel's/ cancer's back. Talking about being a proud grandmother.

The event ended early for us as we left after the survivors' lap around the track. I was very reluctant to try walking, so my husband drove me around the track on the ATV. There were lots of wonderful activities going on, and I was sorry to leave when we did, but I was acutely aware of my limitations.

I left the middle school around 7:00 that Saturday evening, mesmerized by my granddaughter's support of their grandmother and the cause. I left also that evening with a feeling of kinship, having been with so many other people like me, who are trying to live and navigate through cancer. All year long, unless I'm in the cancer center, I am somewhat isolated with this illness. But on that one day, I was surrounded by others like me, finally feeling somewhat normal, as unnatural as that may sound to some. Cancer is far from anything we would want to consider as normal, but it's my normal, whether I like it or not. And to see it existing within others as well removes some of the isolation and boundaries. For a while, I felt in a place of acceptance, and that was so encouraging. The square peg finally had her day with many other square pegs, and we all fit well together. I found this day an additional motivation to fight hard to return to this event again next year.

Silence

Silence is a rarity not easily achieved. Even if we intentionally try, we find it all but impossible. Outside of the obvious noises around us that make silence impossible—TV, radio, computer, traffic, people, animals: the list could go on and on—there are the things we don't think about, like the hum of the heat pump or the refrigerator with all of its moans and groans.

Don't think that by going to the tranquility of the bedroom there will be total silence. Some of us still have the breathing or snoring of our spouse lying beside us. There's the wind blowing, the frogs croaking, or the crickets making incomprehensible sounds right outside of our windows. The walls, windows, and floors are popping. At some time during the night, there most often seems to sound as if someone or something is residing in the attic—just ask any three- to sixteen-year-old kid about that one.

We mustn't think that we could even try to achieve silence outside in what we refer to as "the country life." At any given time, there are more birdcalls in process than even the Audubon can identify. The breeze causes a sway in the trees, creating even more sounds, including the occasional snapping of limbs or falling of one past its expiration. Silence outside also will not come close to being achieved as long as there are ill-tempered squirrels nearby. They always have a lot to bicker about in their own unique language.

So where, then, can silence be achieved in this world we live in? Maybe by putting our fingers in our ears . . . no, that doesn't work either. All this does is allow us the lack of interferences of outside noises so we can better hear the inner works of our own bodies.

I think I will now turn this thought over to the individual reader to ponder for himself—but only if this curiosity is, in his opinion, worth spending time thinking about.

December 21, 2015
The Christmas Cards

Four days before Christmas, I entered the hospital cancer center, where the year before I sat waiting my turn to receive infusion in one of the back rooms. I was often lost in my thoughts that were usually driven by the reality of where I was at that moment. As the memories of my own treatment flooded my mind, I navigated my way to the infusion waiting room to pass out the Christmas cards I carried in my hand.

With only a few cards passed out and the story of their origin conveyed to patients that seemed to all be in some level of despair, I turned to the other side of the room and there it was: the familiar look of disconnect. He stared straight ahead like some of the other cancer infusion patients, almost trance-like. I all too well understood this state of mind that can be present on the day of infusion.

Usually, with that stare there was nothing in the line of sight worth looking at, and it didn't matter because our minds would be so engulfed in our own emotions. These emotions contained in that stare are silent to the world but demanding attention within our own minds.

His stare remained stern until I approached him. He was an older gentleman, much older than me and very white in his complexion. He broke his stare and a smile was forced as our eyes met and I bid him good morning. His smile was met with one of my own, and I began to talk to this man who now sat in the same chair where I'd sat previously. I felt the return of that same apprehension that was ever-present during my infusions, and I was moved with compassion for him. I held out and he received the card, and his smile grew with genuine gratitude.

This man who sat alone lost in his thoughts and disconnected from the environment around him was now engaged in conversation with me, and I saw a spark of joy in his eyes. We talked of how the students in The Leftovers Club in Powhatan County High School were passionate for the people who were going through the battles of cancer, and they were compelled to let these patients know that they are never alone. They had made these cards, and I was honored to pass them out in the cancer centers. They were the evidence of their love and dedication for all who were enduring this disease on this week of Christmas. In this moment, both this man and I felt a connection between a student so many counties away and the two of us. We shared the love that was made evident in the card he now held in his hand.

With the giving and receiving of that special Christmas card, just a little healing was able to take place between us, and the joy that the students intended was realized.

Marjorie

You welcomed me into your home with the warm smile that is you. I can't believe we have lived only two houses apart, and this is the first time I've entered your home—a lovely home with all the warmth and charm that I would have expected. Your eyes looking into mine shone bright with the wisdom and endearment that one would expect from a woman of your maturity. A wisdom and graciousness that presents with such strength.

There is a feeling of ease as I am introduced to your family by taking a pleasurable tour through the many old family photos lovingly arranged throughout the room. What a beautiful family! Each photo is as striking as the one before. I felt privileged to glance into several generations of your heritage, even if only for a moment.

I believe that life moves us around in this world, and that it is up to each of us to discover the reasons why we land where we do at certain times. I believe my reason for landing in this tiny neighborhood where we both live was to meet and get to know you. I have enjoyed each story about your past that you have shared with me and long to hear more. You were from a time when people were kinder and more loyal to one another. Those attributes are still evident in you today.

My friend Marjorie, I would like to thank you for sharing your kindness and glimpses of what your life was like. I wish I had known you earlier in my life.

As I am to move on to the next step in my life story, my journey may take me far away from this home where I now live and thus far away from you, my sweet friend. But know that I go having grown in my faith in humanity from having known you. I will not forget you, and I will carry a confidence with me that we will meet again one day in God's kingdom. Thank you for helping to grow my love for humanity.

Judgment?

As we live our lives to what we perceive as the best of our abilities, we often don't see how we ourselves are handling life. Do we ever fully understand ourselves, much less anyone else? Oh, it is easy to judge someone's actions based on our own expectations. The trick is to understand that those expectations can sometimes be exclusively our own opinion, and not relevant to the person being judged. There are so many different aspects to life, and we could never expect any one person to think or be exactly like ourselves. We must realistically accept that not everyone will agree to share in the same response we might have to the human behavior around us.

I often look for those with bad behavior to be held accountable for their behavior. Then I question myself whether this judgment of accountability is for myself, society, God, or for the person's own good. And by whose standards do I judge their accountability?

Before I become too critical about someone else's behavior, I must first examine my own motivations for such judgment. Am I judging by the pain it causes me, and if so, would I then say it is justified as an unacceptable behavior?

Then I realize this offense may not cause the same pain in someone else's opinion. Where then does the true identity of this behavior lie? In my reasoning, I hold up the behavior to the word of God, and in doing so I try to at least gain understanding of my own intolerance.

Judgment may come from our preconceived standards, society's laws, or the Lord. Which judgment is correct?

The offender will be judging in self-defense and out of the weakness that birthed the offense.

The offended will be judging out of the pain and emotions of the offense.

The law will be judging out of the opinion of the leaders chosen by the masses of society.

The Lord will be judging out of love.

I resolve to release my presumption to assume the burden to judge. I release the responsibility of judgement to the only source worthy to judge, and that is my Lord, the one true judge. Where deemed necessary, the law of the land should prevail. When offended, I may discuss the day-to-day infractions against me with the offender and then focus on recovery. We should mature to trust in a Lord who will see both myself and the person who offended me through this trial. After all, God and Jesus love both the offender and the offended, imperfections and all.

Life is full of these offenses, so I must continue to remember to take the judgment of them to our Lord and allow myself to focus on forgiving. I have always believed that it would be easier to forgive someone else of an offensive action and strive to not have to forgive myself of the same behavior. So, I have lived most of my life in a way as to treat people in accordance with God's word. His word is essential in keeping offenses to a minimum, and in keeping God's word in my heart, I have been able to curtail such offenses easily.

A gaping wound has remained open from the many offenses acted upon me, festering without stitches, until I at last allow the Lord to be those stitches. He can heal the wounds that harbor the pain within me. I must release this pain and forgive for the benefit of us all, and then simply let Jesus do what He does. Only then can I find true resolve and the peace I so desperately seek.

God is love, and His son Jesus shares in that love, and judgments will be made out of that same love, leaving us all with an everlasting hope no matter where we have walked on this earth.

In knowing that God's plan will prevail, I can relax and let the healing from the pain take place, no matter what the offense portrayed upon me was. Our Creator God, and our Savior Jesus Christ, the son of God who took our sins upon Himself, have a love and forgiveness that is greater than any offense committed. All we have to do is believe and surrender to that love. Then we can also find forgiveness in our own heart and achieve the sweet surrender of eternal life and peace.

Friends from My Old Neighborhood

I sometimes think back to a time when I was an active wife and mother in my old neighborhood. Not only was it the old neighborhood where I used to live, but also it was an old neighborhood in its existence. This place where I called home for six years was one that was from a generation older than my own. I loved that charming neighborhood that was built in the '40s and '50s. It reminded me of my childhood neighborhood, where everyone knew everyone, and you could depend on each other for almost everything.

Vegetables were exchanged from one neighbor to the other all season long, and baked goods passed over fences and across roads was almost a competition among us. If any of us would be an egg short of making a cake, a sudden trip to the store wasn't necessary as long as the supply was sufficient in the house next door. Sharing was always welcomed among us all. It simply made life easier.

We would never fret about car repairs being done when we had neighbors willing to lend a ride to wherever we may need to go. We really didn't mind asking for a helping hand when it was needed, because we all truly didn't mind being there for each other. Isn't that the way it's supposed to be?

Since I left that old neighborhood, I have never quite found that kind of comradery again. Once or twice it was notable, but not the same.

When someone was sick or injured, or a death occurred, the entire neighborhood was aware of it, and they sprang into action to take care of every need. These days, many neighbors live isolated from each other, and that increases my longing for those days gone by. I am grateful for the couple of neighbors where I currently live who have reached out during my illness with comfort and support. And still I am perplexed as to where the rest of the neighborhood has been for the last several years. I guess I'm looking for something that was generational, and that to some degree was left behind in that old neighborhood.

In my current condition struggling with a terminal cancer, a part of the old neighborhood has found its way back to me. Even though I live far away from them now, two of my old neighbors who were dear friends so long ago have returned to my life at this time to support me in my time of need. How rewarding that is to have them support me in so many ways. The memories from the happiest of times in my life have been renewed between us. I am so joyful to see their faces again, along with the help they have offered, and I have appreciated their follow-through. I love the feeling of returning to that most wonderful time when we were raising our children together in that old neighborhood. I renew that feeling each and every time we are together.

Ann and Kathy, thanks for taking me back to a more innocent time by making your presence known to me today. It has truly made a positive difference in my search to find peace in this trying time of my life. The value of our rekindled friendships is priceless.

The Cloudy Day

My soul this morning reflects the dark clouds that consume the sky above me. The rain is a paradox to the tears that have evaded me. The few tears I've wasted over the years have become distant and cease to present themselves. There is an accumulation of sorrow within me.

I am not sorrowful about the decisions I have made or about the relationships that have crossed my path in life. I am, however, sorrowful for the actions of some of those who were in that path and the choices they made and how they affected my life. There seems to be a blindness to hurtful behavior in our society. I do not speak of simple mistakes, which we all are guilty of, but of intentional, premeditated, selfish, deceitful, damaging behavior. I see very few people being held accountable for their vile behavior, therefore signaling to them the freedom to continue, and with no repercussions.

Perhaps I should intensify my resolve for this concern. The overwhelming evidence of the scars that never fully healed has become my burden.

My preoccupation with these thoughts exhausts me and drains the precious energy that then becomes unrightfully lost. There are reminders all around me of the emotions I so desperately try to avoid, and I muster all my sanity to combat these thoughts.

I understand that these offenses take hold of my mind only because I allow them to. I must continue to replace these thoughts with the thoughts of the goodness that becomes evasive when the negative thoughts prevail. The beautiful things in life have remained in my mind, but, unfortunately, they reside there as a minority. It's just a matter of disciplining my mind to control where I allow my thoughts to linger.

I now reserve the right to focus on the sunny, warm day forecasted for tomorrow, spawning the potential warming of my spirit, thus eliminating the melancholy that the dark clouds have presented me with today. The evasive tears will essentially be deemed unnecessary in the presence of the renewed hope I will consciously embrace. The sun *will* come out tomorrow, so I'll hang on till tomorrow.

Thank you, Annie.

The People of Migration

Our grandparents, time having now thrust them forward into being called great-grandparents, are also known as the Greatest Generation. The primary reason for such an honorable description was their overwhelming ability to overcome the toughest of situations and remain strong without the assistance of Prozac. That is amazing by modern standards. They survived World War II and the Great Depression and still managed to live a reasonably normal productive life. Amazing.

However, there is a new phase to so many in this remarkable generation who many overlook and that is their autumn migration south every year. I watched this happen with my neighbors and dear friends, the Shorts. Every year at the exact same time, they would clean and load a fifteen-plus ton RV and head to Florida.

Now, what makes this migration so remarkable is that these elderly people, usually small in stature and either sporting gray, silver, blue, or white hair, would get behind the wheel of a home bigger than the one they would escape to for the winter, and actually drive hundreds of miles. No fears of what could happen with the fatigue of an eighty-five-year-old on the highway trying to control a house on wheels on the same highway as a Fiat. They have already overcome so much that even their extended age does not deter them from what they set their minds to.

Some could even drive up to a thirty-TON!!! 510 horse-power diesel engine home to Florida and do this successfully. Every situation in life has its own catastrophes with no exceptions, but for the most part this geriatric population can still cut the mustard.

Hats off to what remains of the Greatest Generation, who also successfully navigate their way back home in April, only to jump out of the RV, unpack, grab the tiller, and start tilling the dirt out back of their humble home so they can raise the vegetables necessary to stock the RV for the return trip in autumn to Florida once again.

We are often taught not to look back at the past, but to look forward; however, in this example of courage and perseverance, I want to look back at as many of their experiences as possible. I do this with a longing to have been a part of their world that produced so many wonderful, self-confident, and courageous people. We should never let what's left of them go unnoticed.

Invitation

You are invited to: A Pity Party

Date: Today or perhaps another day spontaneously

Time: Right now, but only lasting about five minutes

Place: Any mode used to hear my voice

Never mind. I'm over it.

Maybe Later

Maybe sometime later today, I will think about just how beautiful the world we live in really is. I will talk with a calmness that is reassuring and smile that smile that you love to see.

Maybe sometime later today, I will run that errand, do that chore, or make that call. I'll once again hold my head up and pretend that I'm doing far better than I actually am.

Maybe sometime later today, I will write another story and release an idea I've been retaining inside my head, and then relax in self-satisfaction.

But right now, I will allow myself to be where I actually am. I am tired, I am hurting, I feel sick, I am a bit frightened, and I am alone. Only sometimes am I comfortable with feeling the things that are defining me, and only for a while, before I must return to a more socially acceptable definition as to how I feel. "I'm okay," I often say, regardless of how bad I may feel on that particular day. Today's okay was yesterday's ER visit. Now that's a definitive change.

Maybe sometime later today, I will at least put on the appearance that I am much better than I actually am to those around me, proclaiming to feel better—that what I'm really feeling may be a bit difficult to live up to, but it's not necessarily a bad thing.

Get Over It!
Really?

I approached this topic after having a deep discussion with my husband, and in deep meditation and prayer with our God, the God that is known to the world as the God of love. This is a topic that I have been struggling with for a while now, and I long for resolve, not only for myself but also for many others around me and throughout the world who are struggling and even suffering with this same topic. Grief. There I said it, and it's not a four-letter word, but it's almost treated like one. Grief is a natural part of life for every human being and some in the animal world. If we do not grieve for the close losses around us, then something is missing in our souls.

Grief is not just pertaining to death, but it also exists with other situations that present themselves in our lives. Many people will approach us at what they perceive is the appropriate time during our grieving and tell us that the time is here for us to "get over it." This phrase has become too haphazard these days, and I'm tired of so many getting on the bandwagon of assuming the responsibility of being your psychological savior. I accept that this expression does exist, but it has become too expansive, stepping outside of its boundaries and engulfing areas in our lives where it is hurtful and inappropriate.

Do I sound a bit angry? Well, that's because I *am* angry. I'm angry because some of these people around me are sinking deeper into their despair with this fashionable remark being thrust at them, making them feel as if there is something wrong with them because they can't get over some type of trauma that has struck deep within their hearts. More often it can be the tender and loving hearts that can't just get over it. What gives anyone the authority to think that they can dictate when or how someone should get over tragedies?

We honestly should never ever tell people who are suffering to get over it. We should instead comfort this person and listen attentively to them, then they can begin to release the feelings they are holding in their hearts and in turn begin to heal in a natural way. Most often, we can't fully understand where this person is in their grieving. The timeframe of these emotions is not to be judged by someone on the outside. We are all different, and no one person can or should compare himself with the person in front of him that is grieving. We most often have no authority to judge them.

It's okay that they are not over it at this given time and sometimes maybe not ever truly over it, but what should matter is how they can live with the impression that lingers within the person grieving. They can take their closeness to their particular situation and learn to use this experience to grow themselves and possibly even make a difference in another person's life that is suffering from the same loss. Attach meaning to the loss and then this memory they cannot release can eventually inherit a purpose that will allow them to heal and move forward. But this doesn't always come easy for everyone, and for some, this resolve can remain evasive their entire life. And that in itself may somehow hold purpose. Even still, it is not our place to forcefully judge but instead support them.

Christianity is the perfect example of what I am trying to say. Jesus suffered at the hands of the Roman soldiers and also at the cross where He died. He was risen from the grave, and He once again left the disciples with His ascension to heaven. What if the disciples had been told at some point that they should just *get over* this Jesus thing and move on with their lives? Suppose they would have done just that. Would Christianity have been birthed? They wrote of His life and His death and His sacrifice and were willing to die for His purpose; it doesn't sound like they just got over Him, but instead they carried Him with their every thought throughout every day until their death.

There is a profound difference within the people who can stand up for that purpose that is endowed within them forever. A purpose that came about through their grieving.

We should be careful to never say such hurtful words as (get over it) to grieving persons, as it sounds so derogative. I plead to all to work toward replacing it with the courage within us to share with the person in need. We should explore the possibilities that can evolve into a new purpose where they are currently standing. We can do this through our support, ideas, and prayer. Then the healing can commence without "getting over it," but rather gaining acceptance and purpose for their situation and for the life *they* choose to live.

Perhaps

So now it has come to this. With more and more of my body succumbing to the cancer, my existence in normal life has all but dissipated. I mostly go from my bed to the recliner that sits in the double front window in what used to be our dining room. Here I sit and watch the outdoors, which I am so fond of. The bugs and bees along with the birds and blue-tailed lizards coexist in the border of flowers and bushes outside the window where I currently reside with my miseries. I share in the enjoyment that these creatures find in my flowers of pink, orange, and yellow. The sunflower hangs its head lowly today as the bees continue to visit its bloom. The hummingbirds fight amongst themselves for the sweet nectar of the two hanging, bright red feeders. In the same arena exist the two bird feeders filled with seeds that attract most of the native birds to my community.

My writing has become scarce, as I lack the strength or desire to do hardly anything anymore. The simplest of tasks necessary to survive have become forceful encounters. Oh desire, why must you cater to this disease and partake in its destruction of my life?

Time has wandered away from me, and now I have arrived at the stage of cancer that I have always projected as being far away. I am exceptionally ill at this moment and struggle to hold on to a hope that seems to be dangling by a thread. And still I foster the thought that a miracle may one day soon intervene on my behalf. Perhaps.

Sharing My Life with Ann

A typical Monday morning after what was another less than desirable night last night. When I am finally able to pull myself out of bed, and the deficit that my body holds me in, I reach for my phone and contemplate to whom might I place a much-needed SOS call. With options running short considering most people are at work on any given Monday morning, I narrow my list. And then I realize that one of the most important people in my life just happens to be available to call. My friend of many years, Ann, is who one might consider a sound piece of the foundation of friends that can be depended on. We are connected in such a way that sometimes we can almost speak each other's words before we say them ourselves. She is the most likable person I have ever known in many ways. We lift each other up in a way that Christ always intended us to do as sisters in Christ.

That phone call is often made on those difficult mornings, and most often her voice resounds on the other end of my phone. On occasion, our conversation can go on until we have covered almost every topic known to womanhood. I truly believe we always come out of those phone calls in a better place than before we talked.

"My buddy" is her closing endearment for me both on the phone and text, and it tickles me that we are buddies. And this buddy is helping me with the pain of my illness as well as moving away from the pain of those who have hurt me in the past.

I am eternally grateful for her dedication to our friendship and her creativeness and willingness to help me in this time of need. I am blessed beyond my expectations for Ann and several other friends for letting me see the love that is achievable in humanity while still on this earth. We are all given a choice as to how we affect the lives around us, and Ann has been one of those who weaves a web of love everywhere she goes. I consider myself fortunate to have gotten myself caught up in this web of love.

Isolation

I awake to another morning of solitude in the world of cancer. I'm so desperate to live before I die, and yet I find no resolve to get out more. Cancer is rendering me unable to drive due to pain and fatigue. Some of those I hunger to be with cannot or will not visit me. I don't want to overexert the very few who do give me some of the attention required at this time, and I resist reaching out to people I don't know or hardly know. I feel I am an inconvenience or a burden, so I mostly refrain from asking for help because I continue to feel the sting of the rejections already encountered.

What happened to taking the initiative and just being there without having to be asked? Everyone knows there are needs every terminally ill person is faced with, but so many do not want to interrupt their own lives to inherit any responsibilities for those needs.

I really don't feel like writing about this again, but I am consistently revisiting this topic in my life, making it one of the overwhelming thoughts in need of resolution. Life is cruel to have landed so many people in this needy position where we get to see the true hearts of so many around us, and too often it is disappointing. I am disheartened.

Whatever the relationship people have with a terminally ill person, we all do inherit a responsibility to be compassionate toward them, and yet in these days most ignore what their own eyes show them. It is very sad to say, but in today's world many people are so caught up in day-to-day life they cannot see the need around them and cannot see past their own wants.

I am sad as I face another day alone, afraid to reach out, afraid of being rejected again. The excuses are vast and often trivial, but they are theirs to use, and I must accept them. So I sit alone, looking out the window again at the trustworthy birds outside my window. Retrieving my own meals and attempting to do a few things I know I'm not supposed to do. I attempt them for my own self-preservation and because I want to do them. I'm entitled to a few, however small, achievements throughout the day while I can still at least try, right?

An Actual Reality in My Mind

Reality . . . is most often left to the interpretation in each of our minds. Sometimes acceptance of our own interpretations is influencing the reality of what's being played out right before our eyes. What role does intellect, misunderstanding, and denial play in those interpretations? Also, how does each of us compartmentalize the things that appear to hurt us the most when accepting our own realities? Could what we believe to be a reality change its actual form within our mind simply by our own will? With our will, maybe unwanted realities can sometimes no longer exist with prominence in our minds. They can become shadowed, then converted to become something more acceptable by our own standards. How does each of us turn off the pain that sometimes comes with life? Finding this ability can be essential for some of us as we are faced with extreme stresses.

I must deny the reality of my pain, the betrayals right before me, and the mistrust that exists in my actual reality. I must replace the insanity of these hurtful realities with the substitutes conjured to replace the actual reality. I must replace them in order to sustain my own sanity. I have learned to alter the pain within my mind. I will sometimes find solace by settling my mind with fictitious excuses for the bad behavior I have witnessed and try to accept that hurtful behavior. And then I will survive another day.

This necessary acceptance does not exist in my heart and soul but only in my thoughts. The hurt of this world I will to not travel with my spirit—that spirit which is within me, and with which I have always been in touch. I am, however, unaware as to what will be retained within my spirit upon its departure. And whereas no one knows for sure what life experiences remain within our spirit, I do desire that only the beautiful moments of my life will be engraved within my spirit in eternity and that if any of the sadness and pain remains with me, it will fade away in my new existence in the love of God's kingdom.

I search for understanding as to where the hurtful and disrespectful behavior originally came from within the people who hurt me so. Was it from the pains of the perpetrator's childhood, an addiction, a disorder within the brain, or perhaps from within their soul? I can sympathize with the hurting child within them, and in turn, restructure my own pain to better accept their behavior, if that be the reasoning. An addiction should have been addressed a long time ago, and this reasoning causes me still more rationalizing to ignore my own pain. A brain disorder may be beyond their or my control, so I just try to suppress its existence the same as them and rise above the pain. If the meanness is from their soul and that is the reason it exists, then my heart holds on to the truth of that pain, and so I must deny my heart.

Is there a reasonable interpretation that would shift the bad realities? Does this defense in self-preservation make sense? It has worked to sustain me through many years of pain, most of which was inflicted on me intentionally. Where is this erroneous behavior in the thought process of the offending person? Or is it the lack of such processing in their minds that sanctions such continual substandard behavior? Their own endorsement of this behavior is the same reality as the resistance I hold for their behavior within my own mind. Thus, I must as usual be the one to find understanding and in turn forgiveness, no matter the duration of their trifling actions. However, every time I offer forgiveness, they gain power over me.

Even with the vast population of people who find blatant meanness a way of life, there are still those who lift the people around them with goodness that is sustainable and healing. And I am eternally and internally grateful to those blessed people who have stepped into my life. The light of these beautiful people burns even brighter in the darkness that the contemptable people created.

Good and evil has existed in humanity since the beginning of our existence. During this duration of good and evil, there has been an inherent difference between the two, other than the obvious. And that is the difference in how people retain life experiences in their consciousness. One of the two seems to be lacking a mindful consciousness, thus allowing such dreadful behavior.

Tolerance will become our own demise one day. Our not rationalizing where that threshold bends or even breaks has given credence to evil, allowing it to gain far too much control in a world that was designed to be loving and peaceful. My heart pangs. I've seen far too much wrongdoing in my lifetime, both personal and in the world every day. And it has exhausted my gentle soul.

These thoughts I have as I am dying were never intended to be revealed, and yet here they are before me, recorded and left behind. I write these thoughts with a hope of purging them out of my mind, heart, and soul. I put them on these pages in search of a freedom away from their relevance. I can't believe that this life has been visited by so much evil that such thoughts have been prevalent in my mind so often for so many years. Does any human have the right to cause such destruction to someone else's peace? Not in my reality, but perhaps in theirs. And so, I will continue to endure until I release my spirit with the death that we all must encounter, whether good or bad. On that day, the one true reality will be revealed.

March 8, 2016
Exactly 1:00 pm

The deck on the back of our home hasn't been maintained. After all, we must not break with tradition. My husband is in charge of all maintenance at his work eight hours a day, so traditionally he must neglect our own property when he returns each day to his own home. I think maybe this is some sort of unwritten law.

For *some* reason, our grungy deck enticed the most beautiful bird of song this morning. It was a familiar song to the spring season. This pleasing little bird's song took me back to springs as distant as my childhood. One could almost taste and smell the season at hand through this enchanting bird's song. A bit repetitive but beautiful.

Spring, in this girl's opinion, belongs to the birds and blooms. Spring is yellow, blue, purple, green, white, red, and pink all around me. Sunshine can finally be fully felt. No matter where I've been in my life, this season shows its renewal of life. You cannot be alive and not feel the hope that spring represents.

Chocolate bunnies accompanied with assorted candy eggs, Peeps, and jelly beans fill children's Easter baskets, while well-dressed adults and children alike, some in bonnets, accompany each other to church for Easter resurrection services. Another reason for hope in this beautiful and warm season.

I am grateful for this little bird's announcement this morning. He masterfully chirped proclamation of all that this season has to offer and will continue in the weeks to come. I plan on being a part of it.

Petie

I don't remember a lot about Petie except for this one particular warm spring day back when I was a very young child. I can guestimate my age to be about four or five years old. Our parakeet, Petie, lived in a small cage that often swung back and forth on its metal stand. The metal stand that held Petie's cage always stood in the same place day after day, and that place was in our tiny kitchen right next to the side window.

Mama would often scold Petie, to no avail, when he was being too noisy during meals. My sisters, brother, and I would often stick our small fingers through the void spaces in between the tiny metal rods that made up Petie's cage, hoping for some kind of response from our only pet. He most often let us down with his lack of interest in our wiggling fingers.

I can remember that a caged bird was not exactly the most exciting of pets for small children, but we loved him because, after all, he was our little Petie.

On that particular day, Mama let Petie out to fly around for a while in the house. This was a rarity for Petie, and it brought about an air of excitement amongst us children watching him flutter about the house. Petie would land on the highest items in the house when a rest was needed. He would perch on a curtain rod or the top of a picture frame hanging on the wall. As I recall, he also landed on the edge of the hanging ceiling light.

As time passed, we lost our interest in this bird who was now tiring of his freedom. He resolved to perch outside of our reach, so we turned our attention to playing outside. We exited the house through the backdoor, where Petie had been apparently planning his escape. Only two of us four children were out the door when it happened so quickly. Petie flew high above our heads, but low enough to set himself free through the open screen door.

We never thought that Petie would contemplate leaving his home where he was loved so much, but obviously he was just biding his time till he could escape. In our confusion, we didn't really see in what direction he departed our company.

Mama seemed both furious that we let the bird fly past us and frightened for his safety in a world he was not familiar with. We all spent the better of that day calling and searching for Petie. The more time that passed, we were losing hope that Petie would return to us.

When evening at last rolled around, we could feel a nip of cold in the air and became very concerned for him. I remember becoming very upset that Petie was truly gone from us forever and that he very well may not survive the cool nights still present in early spring.

Mama grabbed the clothes basket to retrieve the laundry that had dried on the clothes line hanging in the backyard when we all heard her excitement. She pointed towards the clothes line in the distance, and there was Petie, perched between two clothespins that were holding the now-dry tablecloth.

Mama calmly told us to freeze in our tracks and remain behind, as she would attempt to approach our little green bird perched on the top of that colorful tablecloth. Mama stealthily tippy-toed toward the timid, little bird. Whether or not she was stealthy to Petie that day, it worked. Before we knew it, our beloved bird was in Mama's hands, almost as if his adventure was over, and now he was ready to return to his cage in our warm house.

Mama walked swiftly back to the house and through the back door with Petie secure in her hands. A moment later, she returned to the backyard and announced to us that Petie was safely in his cage. We were elated with Petie's return to our home and asked if we could unfreeze now. Mama laughed and gave us all permission to unfreeze.

We all headed to the back porch, obeying Mama's command to do so. But before we went inside, Mama explained to all four of us how it was that our Petie was able to find his family once more. You see, Petie had sat in his cage all day every day, just few feet away from that tablecloth with its many colors, and Mama believed that when he became cold and longed for his warm cage, he looked about and saw the familiar tablecloth. Petie perched on that tablecloth hanging on the clothesline in hopes of finding his safe cage, and indeed it did save him from the cold night and bring him safely home.

I wonder still today if we would have ever seen Petie again had Mama not washed that tablecloth and hung it to dry on the clothesline that day. I was grateful for that colorful tablecloth, and I'll never forget the little green bird named Petie that seemed to be much smarter than we had given him credit for.

The Divisions of America

We don't even need to turn on the television or the internet to see all the divisions that are happening in the United States and all over the world. However, these two resources tend to contribute immensely to each and every division present. In fact, I do not hesitate to say that media is the fuel of choice in feeding the fires within these divisions.

So many people are a willing or an unwilling part of the race divisions—something that I believe we could all get past one day if the media wasn't so antagonistic.

The haves and the have nots. They have always existed and in all likelihood always will. No need for the media to flame the fires of division. Wealth versus poverty has been present since the early recording of humanity. I am hesitant to think that this will ever really be resolved. Some may proclaim they know the answers to this division, but they never deliver any plausible resolve or resolution.

Educational boundaries are ever-present and cause a blindness to great talents. Not everyone has the funds or life situation that is conducive to obtaining a higher education. Yet many positions are only filled by people who can obtain degrees, a great choice but not the only choice. Many great minds are left by the wayside and never given a chance. Sometimes the loss is greater with the employers, those who are not willing to open their eyes and see *who* is before them instead of just *what* is before them.

The next division I speak of needs no explanation, and that's the fierce, competitive division between sports teams. If we had half of the time and money back that is regularly being spent on this division, we could resolve many the problems that are staring us in the face.

Another division before our eyes is, of course, the division between political parties, almost identical to the last division mentioned. Whether or not your side is right or wrong, or winning or losing, one most often seems to stick to the party. In my opinion, not always the best idea. I probably should just stop right here on this one, because I could go rounds on this phenomenon for far too long.

Cat lovers versus dog lovers. Animal rights versus human rights, and believers versus non-believers. That's enough for anyone to get the picture. I'm sure there are many more, but I will leave that to the reader. We are divided in more ways than a sliced pie in a cheap café.

Enter the division that is present, often even in one household. The division that sometimes cannot be resolved, even in the best of relationships. Most often, if the debate is started between any two people, it is ended in a gridlock. Seldom will either side give in to defeat as to which side is better. However, I must say that within my own home, after several years of living with this division, my husband and I finally came together. My husband and I are now one. Our division no longer exists. And he is happy with his conversion. We enjoy a simpler partnership these days and are able to better share in each other's little worlds.

This final division that I speak of is relatively new to the world, but a division just the same. Spoken of often in homes, classrooms, restaurants, cafés, and almost everywhere, it won't go away, and even though it is a division among us, it is usually a peaceful division that we can live with.

So, might the reader have guessed what this everyday, simple but recognizable division is? I'm almost hesitant to reveal that which I am speaking of. I have truly enjoyed leaving those who have not figured this out already hanging. In conclusion, here it simply is: iPhone vs Android. Oh, my goodness, you have got to agree. It's all around us, and it's a peaceful division. Here's to the saga of the cell phone gorge dug in between us all. Lol!

Sunday with Kathy

Having had new neighbors build and move in just beyond our house and in plain sight, at least by rural standards, I moved my writing hangout away from the front of my house. This I did to allow both them and me more privacy. You see, I spend the better part of my day sitting right in front of my big living room window, watching over the field across the gravel road in front of my house while I complete a large sum of writing.

Recently, there has been a great deal of human activity in the field in front of my house and an assorted array of vehicles driving back and forth on the gravel road. And whereas I'm usually feeling pretty sick, I would normally be sitting there in my pajamas. Needless to say, this little world as I know it is in need of a change. So, I say goodbye to the usual critters that I on occasion would watch perform in the field across the street, and I moved to the back of the house in the sunroom.

I will miss the ventures of the groundhog that lived in the drain pipe at the end of my driveway. There were almost always hawks scouring the field for mice. Turkeys would sometimes number over a dozen—and every year since we first moved here, there have been young deer families grazing in the field. I would often watch the youngest of them emerge from the woods for the first time and hang cautiously at the edge of the woods as they grazed.

Now I sit in my new domain in the back of my house with my computer in front of me and wonder what to write this Sunday afternoon. There is but one thought in my head, and that is a visit from an old friend, Kathy, who is from my old and favorite neighborhood. I have been anxiously watching the clock almost constantly all morning long. The hours I have been counting down have turned into minutes now that the hour has passed twelve. My friend texted me yesterday that she would be here by 1:00. As I write this, it is 12:10, so she will arrive soon.

I retreat from this part of the page and work out some editing on the previous paragraphs, and now as I return my glance to the clock, it tells me my friend is due to arrive in just fifteen minutes. I feel as giddy as a schoolgirl at a sleepover. That's how it is with me and Kathy . . . she makes me laugh. There can never be too much of that these days. I will quit writing now and go back to the front of my house and watch for her arrival. This will be one of the exceptions for being in that front window. After all, I am fully dressed today, leaving no room for someone to pass by and see me in my pajamas.

The hours have passed by, and friend has since left my home to return to her dedicated husband waiting a county away. I now return to my keyboard, where I am left to reflect on our visit today. This a visit of five hours of fulfilling conversation.

On this day, the twentieth of March, it feels as if we have returned to the dead of winter, thus leaving us with little alternative other than remaining indoors, where we found engaging in conversation to be the logical choice for our time spent together today. And we were correct in that logic, as this day brought a plethora of topics, all explored in depths normally unattainable in mundane everyday, passive conversations.

I will hold dear to me this time spent together, connecting as two friends, mothers, and grandmothers—stories shared in confidence sometimes with tears and moments of laughter and surprises that fulfill the need we so often have for this kind of human compassion.

I feel very blessed that our friendship has survived the test of time, and that the two of us have retained an appreciation for each other. Five hours of my life well spent on this Sunday afternoon. I hope it was as rewarding for this appreciated friend of mine as it was for me.

Love of Life

I think at times that I have loved life more than it has loved me.

Tonight, my skin tingles fiercely, and it feels as if needles are piercing most of my body. My chest feels as if it has been ripped open by a bear. Not just any bear, but a grizzly bear. My head and ears hurt, and I am, to say the least, not at all comfortable. It's one of those nights that I am desperately clinging on to life while considering the will of letting go. Thus far, the clinging on continues to win in that tug of war.

It's our love of life that helps build the endurance necessary to overcome the feelings that come with a terminal diagnosis. It's what we do as humans: *live*—so we fight to do what we do best. We are all trying to stay alive in some way each and every day, only with some of us, that effort is much harder to achieve.

I sit at my window this morning, watching the lot next to my home being cleared in preparation for a new home to be built. In the midst of all the noise of the machinery, I am a silent witness to all the tall beautiful trees that have lost their lives and fallen to the ground. Being the thirtieth of October, the trees are coated with golden, orange, and red leaves. They are beautiful, falling to the ground with all the brightly-colored leaves intertwining in the air and the sun illuminating them. I accept this momentary beauty but feel the great loss of these trees on this day.

I think we must consider ourselves as these fallen trees I sit and observe today, beautiful and purposeful. Their purpose to stand their ground seems to me to be as powerful as our own, but still the day comes for everything and everyone to fall. Today is their day, but not mine.

The destruction of these trees continues as the day moves on. The projected outcome is a new dwelling, which will emerge from the clearing for a young family to live out their lives.

Purpose has its dominion over endurance,
and the lot is cleared by nightfall.

Rusty

Although it may appear otherwise, Norma actually wrote this piece. We had several dogs over the years and we both loved them. One day while we were talking she told me that I should get a four-legged friend when she went home to be with our Lord. I am not very outgoing or social kind of guy so I guess she knew that I would need a friend here to talk to and care for. Other than church, the kids and grandkids, I spend my time in our home with all of her touches and all of her things; and that brings me comfort. She is a remarkable woman and I cannot begin to tell you how very much I miss her and how very much that I love her. This story is pretty amazing that she picked the dog and his name for me. I remember the day she wrote this piece and knew then and there one day I would have a Rusty in my life. I will fulfill my promise to her and one day adopt a Rusty!... Richard

Rusty was a ward of the county pound when I first met him. I took notice of his long, shiny, golden coat with hints of red. "Cage 26" was written above the door that contained this innocent-looking dog. Also displayed there was the name, Rusty. That name seemed to be appropriate for him considering the coat he inherited had the appearance of the patina of old rusty metal.

The pound was loaded to its fullest capacity that day, but Cage 26 held my attention, which halted my progression through the rest of the pound. You see, this slight, rusty-colored dog seemed to be trying to cuddle with a sleeping bulldog in the cage next to him. He would paw at the cage a bit where the bulldog was lying, then lay as close to the other dog as the cage would allow. Not being able to feel the companionship of the dog next door to him, this lab retriever mix would stand and repeat the procedure over and over again, obviously hoping for a better outcome each time. I thought how lonely he seemed, a feeling I could relate to. You see, I lost my wife to cancer many months ago and suffered the same loneliness observed in this dog before me, in cage number 26.

My quest for companionship seemed to parallel this dog, so I now find myself signing adoption papers for him. "So, Rusty it is," I spoke to this seemingly-obedient dog as our eyes seemed to be locked on one another now that he was finally on the outside of Cage 26.

I reached out, papers completed, to retrieve the flimsy leash provided me to escort my new dog to my home. I came to this little venture ill prepared, not having a leash of my own, so any kind of leash was appreciated. However, the pretty 1960s flower power flowers that adorned it would warrant an immediate trip to Walmart for something a bit more appropriate for this dog I now called my own.

Wherever Rusty came from, I could see that he had evidently been accustomed to riding in cars with his lack of hesitation in boarding the passenger front seat. I rounded the front of the car, taking notice of Rusty's head following my path all the way to the seat I occupied next to him. So as not to rush too quickly into traffic, I took a few moments to look this dog in his face and vigorously rub him behind his ears. Time well accepted by my new companion. Years have quietly passed since I last owned a dog, and I had forgotten how appreciative a lonely dog like Rusty could be. "That's right, boy; it's just us two old dogs now. What do you think about that?" This must have met with his approval also, because I found myself wiping the sloppy kiss that a dog this size gives from my face. "I guess everything is official now that you've licked my face, so let's go home, boy," I said, laughing.

We found our way home uneventful, except for the two times Rusty tried to sit in my lap. I think after shooing him away for his actions both times, he got the message, because he spent the remainder of the trip settled down looking out the passenger and dash windows. "Good looking and smart. I guess I made a good choice in choosing you today, Rusty," I complimented him.

After the necessary bathroom break for Rusty in the backyard, I unlocked the front door, and we both entered what Rusty could now call his home. "Good dog," I praised him as I noticed he did not run and jump on the sofa nor my favorite recliner. Rusty stuck by my side as if he was a bit apprehensive of his new surroundings. By sticking right beside me, he was showing his trust in me, and that was a rewarding start to our new life together.

I looked into my new pet's trusting face and knew that he was just that: a pet. Not a replacement for the love I have lost with the passing of my wife, but something different. Rusty was to be my four-legged pal, and we would fill that void that we both seemed to be feeling. I will most likely never know Rusty's story as to how he wound up alone, but he has a companion now that has learned in life how it is to be dedicated. I guess you could say Rusty is a lucky dog, and I have a feeling I got lucky in getting him also.

"Well, my friend," I spoke softly to this calm dog, "I guess I'll get you a blanket out of the closet for your bed tonight until we can buy all the necessities a dog may need tomorrow." I truly didn't think this thing through before heading to the pound, I thought while shaking my head and heading into the kitchen. "How about a bite to eat?" I asked the dog, who was obviously feeding off of my excitement. I retrieved the platter of yesterday's baked chicken and the veggies of that day out of the fridge. "I guess a little chicken won't do you any harm once in a while," I spoke to him as he beckoned toward the platter of chicken. I pulled off what seemed the correct portion of chicken for a dog his size and knew that I had become his best friend for life with the lowering of that bowl to the floor.

Before I could prepare my plate and beverage and sit at the table, Rusty had finished his meal, much what I expected from a dog just coming out of the pound. My memory had escaped me, as I should have held his meal to dine with me, but I didn't, so I had to pay for this mistake with his pathetic stare directly on my eyes as I ate. I did, however, remember not to start evoking bad behavior, and I ate my meal without guilt from the manipulations of a dog who is smarter than most people would give credit to.

Rusty patiently sat by my side while the dishes were washed and the kitchen once more tidied up. We then took what was to be our final walk in the backyard and headed back toward the house. My head moved side to side, no longer paying attention to Rusty but instead taking survey of the yard that would have to be fenced in for Rusty's outdoor ventures. I was getting too old to be at the beck and call of a dog's bathroom needs. "Come on, boy, let's get her locked up," I said as we entered the house and I threw the bolt to the back door.

Rusty intuitively knew the blanket tossed on the floor was his to do with as he pleased, because as we both entered the living room, he started to adjust it to his liking without any reservations. "Great, I like a dog with confidence who knows what's his," I told him, and took my rightful place in my recliner. We looked for a moment at each other with an unspoken understanding of each other's domain in the living room—an understanding between a dog and his owner that seemed at that moment to be bonding. As our look was now approaching a staring contest, I felt compelled to confess to this dog that I had just held more dialogue with him than this house had heard in a long time. "Maybe tomorrow, I will tell you all about the woman I loved and how she passed away from me. Maybe I'll take you to see where her body rests after we leave the Walmart tomorrow. What do you say boy?" And with that, Rusty rose from his newly-formed bed and approached me, and we exchanged affirmations.

I thought of you, my love, that night as I approached sleep and was sure you would have approved of ole Rusty, even of the way he arranged his makeshift blanket bed. I thought once again of your laughter and knew you would have laughed at his serious attempts to make a perfect bed. Staring into the darkness and seeing your face once again gave me the comfort I needed to rest that night.

The Day Has Come

So, is this supposed to be the beginning of the end? I'm on my fourth day of not being able to control the pain. And the pain I have come to know these last few days is quite a bit more pronounced than that I was accustomed to. I find myself having to resist the tendency to slip into a state of fear, rightfully so. I have learned through this experience that it is not easy being allotted the time to know that I am dying. I am a deep thinker, and I know that I am reaching a level of pain that eventually only death can relieve.

I have had over three years to prepare for this, and yet I lie here frightened at the very thought of going to the next step. I am now forced into having to take the very drugs that my doctors have historically told me not to ever take. I know the risk I will be inheriting and the consequences that I may suffer, but the pain must now somehow be controlled beyond simply utilizing my own tenacity. My ability to function has become impaired, and I am surely suffering now, so I may start the long-dreaded narcotic at my palliative care doctor's office tomorrow.

I have always been enthralled with intelligent thoughts, as I cling to each and every one, and I would like to continue to contemplate the life around me as I always have, so I resist the element that would cause my retreat from that competence. There must be a part of who I am that would falter on these drugs, which in turn would change the person that I and those around me have come to know—a loss that I must confess may have finally become a necessary reality for me.

I find it so ironic that I have fought going on these drugs with all the courage that I could muster while others will lie, steal, and even kill to get these drugs. I have personally known several of these addicted people, and those experiences have greatly contributed to my resistance to succumbing to them myself. I reason in my own mind that these drugs can at times become highly necessary for the relief of higher levels of pain. I also am glad they are available for the many who need or will need them. It's just that I have spent decades not only resisting them because of my previous negative reactions to them, but also because of the outcome they have presented to several people close to my life. So, I ask all to try to forgive my apprehension as I wrestle with the demons of my past concerning these drugs. I try presently to come into compliance with where I should be in the treatment for my stage four cancer. And I know that I must discipline myself tomorrow and learn yet another lesson of this world of cancer. There are always many things in this world that we must learn to come into compliance with. I tell myself this is just one more of those things.

So maybe today will be the last of my writing, a loss that will truly be suffered. Still, I hope to be able to contradict myself and be able to return to the keyboard with a cognitive mind, where I can continue to feel the freedom I have enjoyed in expressing my thoughts. This has been an acceptance I have greatly resisted for so long, and I will not make any guarantees as to how tomorrow will go.

Lions and Lambs

If there is one thing I have learned throughout this ordeal of fighting this disease known as cancer, it is to finally be brave enough to speak up and be honest about my medical concerns.

Don't get me wrong. I'm not by any means here to bash the many good doctors that care for our medical needs and sometimes save our lives. But there are those doctors who treat us badly and in the process of this behavior show the patient disrespect, often in a time when we need kindness and respect the most. If you are this kind of doctor, then this little story is for you.

Usually there is not time enough for the doctor to see the entire picture and gather all the information needed from the patient. And this often can be not only frustrating for the patient but also lead to an incorrect diagnosis.

We, the patients, understand that appointments are being scheduled sometimes as frequently as five and ten minutes apart. This is not beneficial for us, nor is it safe, considering how quickly these doctors must evaluate, make a decision on diagnosis, and form a treatment.

There are patients who present as if they are a lamb, very quiet and obedient while in the doctor's office. Good luck with that, lambs! Then there are the lions that want to express all their symptoms and their history and ask questions concerning the final results. As a good doctor, you must find the resolve and skill to treat the lions and the lambs.

I have been greatly blessed with so many kind, respectful, and knowledgeable doctors on this difficult path where I have found myself, but I am deeply regretful for the few who not only disrespected me but scared me at times to the point of retreating from medical care. I am not alone. I have talked to others who have had to endure this same experience.

I close by saying that I reiterate once more that I am so grateful for the greater list of who I refer to as "the good guys." And I hold out hope that your numbers will continue to dominate the medical field. I also acknowledge that it is true: there is good and bad in every field. However, I feel that when it comes to hurting and dying people, there is no room for disrespectful doctors or nurses.

Even When It's Difficult

I'm losing the ability to navigate my life, and I am rapidly becoming concerned as to how much longer I can cope. I wish I could just get better, so I could slip away from all of this.

Every day becomes harder to comprehend and to hold on to who I am. I don't want to be contradictive to who I have been, but I must admit some of my attitudes are at risk of slipping into the sorrow that surrounds being terminally ill. Everything about having this cancer has turned out to be different and more than I anticipated.

I have always said that it is not fair that this cancer fight should happen to anyone, and yet now I find *myself* slipping away.

I pray that I do not slip from the ability to pray in the presence of God in these difficult moments. I am currently experiencing a diminishing strength that weakens and exhausts my thoughts. Every day, it becomes harder to sustain my life. *Surely this can't be real*, is my plea. I cry out to Jesus to hold me as I continue to cling to this shred of hope that will never burn out within the exhaustion that is me. I will, however, not hold on so tight to this life that I miss the will of my God. Sometimes it is not the same as that of our own, and we all at some point in this life must look to the glory and salvation ahead of us and not fear.

Even if one day I shall lose my hope, I must not gain fear.

About Norma

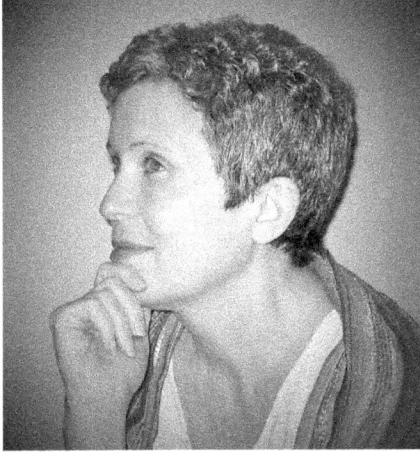

First, I must give this disclaimer: I am a husband, not a writer. I left that up to my beautiful wife, Norma, and how well she did write! My hope is that I can do this narrative justice.

After Norma was diagnosed with a very aggressive form of breast cancer and underwent complex surgery in October 2014, she was given a three-month prognosis. She would later joke that when the three months expired and she didn't, she would write a book—so, she compiled her thoughts and feelings while fighting pain, chemotherapy, and radiation treatments, and her first book, *Impressions Behind the Pink Ribbon*, followed in 2015.

The treatments had no effect on the cancer as genomic testing later disclosed, and, in fact, we learned that her form of cancer had no treatment available. The treatments did however afford her some relief from the pain.

During this time, she was able to get back to her passion of writing, and thus, she was able to write this, her second book.

Unfortunately for all of us, in September 2016, after fighting the good fight, Norma went home to be with our Lord, who she loved and faithfully served despite the cancer and other life-long health issues. She had this manuscript ready for the publisher but was unable to see it to fruition. The book you hold in your hand is a testament to her true labor of love.

Norma was very thoughtful, a deep thinker, and she had the gift of common sense, which is rare today. She blessed many lives, lived life to the fullest, and loved everyone . . . regardless. Despite her own suffering, she would reach out to people at treatment centers, stores, or wherever she felt that a kind word, listening ear, or a hug was needed. She actually ministered to another woman on the surgery floor the morning of her own surgery because the other woman was alone and upset.

Despite the pain, she was able to accomplish several things on her bucket list, such as driving a Dodge Challenger SRT8 on the open highway and having multiple book signings, including her favorite, which was held at the Barnes and Noble in Chesterfield County near our home. She was also able to see all nine grandchildren born and see her first book on the Internet in obscure languages.

My hope is that you found comfort, peace, faith, encouragement, laughter, and hope within these pages. I'm sure you have discovered what a remarkable, insightful, and wise woman she was, and I hope you will enjoy reading her first book, *Impressions Behind the Pink Ribbon*, as much as you enjoyed this one. I know you will be blessed by them both.

—Richard

www.ingramcontent.com/pod-product-compliance
Lightning Source LLC
Chambersburg PA
CBHW020914090426
42736CB00008B/638

* 9 7 8 1 9 4 7 8 6 0 4 6 9 *